St. Petersburg
Nights

William Campbell Douglass, MD

Second
Opinion

ISBN 1-885236-06-9

Library of Congress Catalog Card Number
95-067702

Cover design by Elizabeth Bame

Additional copies of this book may be purchased from Second Opinion Publishing for $22.50. Second Opinion Publishing also publishes Dr. Douglass' monthly alternative health newsletter, *Second Opinion*. An introductory subscription to *Second Opinion* is $49 for 1 year, $89 for 2 years. To subscribe or to obtain more information regarding Second Opinion products, please call or write:

Second Opinion Publishing, Inc.
Post Office Box 467939
Atlanta, Georgia 31146-7939
800-728-2288 or 404-399-5617

Dedication

to

Nikolai Chaika

Dear friend,
brilliant physician,
Russian patriot.

Table of ·Contents

Foreword

The Reasons for
My American Revolution

Normally we associate the need for change with the young. As we grow older, we're supposed to shed our wanderlust and take on the mantle of serene wisdom. That may be so in normal times, but these times are far from normal. (And so am I. Call me anything, but don't call me "normal.")

Year in and year out I was growing more disillusioned — which is hard to do for someone who had few illusions to begin with. Each day some new absurdity would reinforce my belief that America had tragically passed a watershed. The country of Thomas Jefferson, of the strong, independent American — the man or woman who would pursue the American Dream — was increasingly difficult to find. The American frontier spirit, based on the spunk and initiative of the individual, was increasingly giving way to government handouts and narrow interest groups looking to make a quick buck off the backs of taxpayers.

From Woodrow Wilson, that self-righteous, ignorant, and egotistical fop, to the self-righteous, ignorant, and egotistical satyr, Bill Clinton, our government has been destroying American independence, replacing it with an all-powerful bureaucracy which despises and fears the vision of our Founding Fathers.

For me, there was no American frontier to conquer, only bureaucratic red tape to suffer. The republic of limited government our Founding Fathers had bequeathed to us was metamorphosizing into a mobocracy, just as Benjamin Franklin feared it would.

Like most Americans, for me the apparent fall of Russian communism was an exciting prospect. Here was the world's largest country now fighting to rediscover freedom. America struggled as a new republic 200 years ago; Russia was about to face the same challenges.

There, I felt, was the opportunity to help build a new system, to help deliver on the many promises we Americans had made to the Russian people. Throw off your communist oppressors and we will help you, we proclaimed. But would we?

We failed to do so in Hungary in 1956; we failed Czecho-Slovakia in 1968. In both instances, brave people faced death fearlessly, but fruitlessly, while waiting for America to come to their aid. But we didn't. Our leaders stood by, while thousands died combatting tanks and missiles with rocks and fists.

I believe that most Americans, if given the opportunity, would gladly help the Russian people. Not with foreign aid, but with the concepts of our original constitutional system, with the production know-how, and with the marketing genius we uniquely possess.

Although liberals like to berate us for our "selfishness," the truth is that we Americans are the most generous people in the history of the world. We are the most sharing, the most caring, the most giving people who ever lived.

I had an opportunity to bring those traits to St. Petersburg. Beneath my ostensible rationale — the need to study medical light therapy — at a barely conscious level was that small voice we all hear. It's a peculiarly American voice — cynical, biting, a voice that says, "put up or shut up."

It was time for me to put up — to take the anger I felt toward *our* government, and channel it in a more positive direction.

Perhaps the best thing I could do for my country was to temporarily leave it, and befriend a new country as it searched for freedom. If Russia does indeed survive as a free republic — I had my doubts then and have even more now — America will benefit.

Besides, I've always believed, when opportunity comes, you've got to take it. This basic philosophy is what drove Europeans to America, and it's what led me to St. Petersburg. So what if I'm not 20 anymore? I'd make up with the sage advice of experience what I might lack in youthful vigor.

Goodbye to the FDA

I'm not sure I fully realized how badly my disillusioned American spirit sought something *positive* to do for others. And my passion for St. Petersburg wasn't uppermost in my mind, either, although I know now it was burning at a deep, almost primordial level.

But I was fully aware of one tragic irony: I would be freer to practice medicine in Russia than I was in America.

Doctors who practice alternative medicine here, those of us who don't buy into the drug-company vision of American health, know that the FDA and the AMA will stop at nothing to destroy our reputations. We have all put up with the investigations, the allegations, the public condemnations. But Gestapo tactics? That's where I draw the line.

Shortly before my Russian *heijra* — during those many days of indecision when seemingly each minute I would change my mind, then change it again (I'm going, I'm not going; I'm going, I'm not going) — a goon squad of federal officials and local police smashed into the offices of my good friend, Dr. Jonathan Wright, in Tacoma, Washington. Guns drawn, agents broke down the doors to the clinic, pushed frightened nurses and employees against the wall, and proceeded to seize or destroy Dr. Wright's records, equipment, and practice.

You need to understand that Dr. Wright had absolutely nothing to hide. He was breaking no laws, violating no protocols, doing nothing of which he was ashamed. Just the reverse!

The agents could have walked in and taken whatever they wanted, but that wasn't the point. They weren't merely seizing medical records; they were trying to *terrorize* part of the medical profession: that part that challenged the dictates of the FDA. They wanted to send a clear message to all holistic physicians that "this could be your fate, too!"

I may be slow, but I'm not totally stupid. To these bureaucrats, the therapy I was doing (photoluminescence) qualifies as voodoo at best. Forget the fact that the technique has a track record stretching back many decades; forget the numerous documented successes with such dread diseases as hepatitis, cancer, and AIDS; forget the desperate need to use photoluminescence to treat the growing number of AIDS patients; forget even that a form of photoluminescence has been approved by the FDA for more than 40 years.

Big Brother is watching — and if he doesn't like what you're doing, you'd better be prepared to face his wrath. I'm not on the FDA/AMA team, so I was in danger. It appalled me that American medicine, aided by bureaucratic regulation, had come to this.

In Russia, on the other hand, photoluminescence therapy is an accepted technique. You don't have to challenge the system to use it. Russian doctors rely on it and use it routinely. Researchers there continue to make refinements with the therapy, adapting it to treat AIDS and many other diseases. (Their success is doubly impressive, considering the horrid, primeval conditions under which their doctors work.)

Let me tell it to you straight: In America I could easily lose my license for using photoluminescence, regardless of its success; in Russia, I could freely examine years of research and work as I pleased to further refine and improve the technology.

As an American citizen, I was forced to leave my country if I wanted to practice medicine as I believe it should be practiced. Are you amazed? Appalled? You should be. I certainly was.

So in June 1992, I left Atlanta, Georgia for the start of my great adventure. On to St. Petersburg!

Introduction

The More It Changes,
The More It Stays the Same

Most recent stories in the Russian and the international press begin something like this: "Although the shortage of food is not absolutely critical yet, the 'free' citizen is still forced to stretch his tight budget to try and stave off starvation with all possible practical measures."

Actually, that was written on January 26, 1918, three months after the Great October Socialist Revolution. Gotcha! Like today, one gets the feeling the writer wasn't sure whether the Russian people were really free or if they were even going to survive the next winter.

Things haven't changed very much in the past 77 years.

I have gotten a wealth of material from the Russian free press, but sometimes it is difficult to understand exactly what they are trying to say. Take this gem as an example; it's a report in a Russian newspaper on mealtime in our country:

> Now I know the reason for the abundance of food in America: local people consume little of it. A typical American would peck at the peas on his/her plate, with a fork, ignoring a huge schnitzel by the side, sip [cranberry] "juice" and chat for half an hour — calling that "lunch."

From the standpoint of hundreds of years of Russian history, that article actually makes sense. Starvation or near starvation is as common a phenomenon in Russia as food surpluses are in capitalist America. A Russian will eat everything in sight; no other response to food is conceivable.

Along with Dr. Nikolai Chaika, my guardian seagull (Chaika means seagull), I was amused at some of the wonderfully whimsical and lyrical names I encountered in Russia. During my travels I met Doctor One Penny (Kopayka), Mr. Christmas (Rozhdestvo), Martina Magpie (Soroka), Count White Village-White Lake (Beloselsky-Belozersky), Director Coo-Coo Bird (Kukushkin), Dr. Mighty (Maguchi), Dr. Pencil (Karandashov), and my two personal favorites, Dr. Socks (Noske — not the White House cat) and the Symphony Director, Mr. Not Necessary (Nenadovskee), who was not merely necessary, but essential.

The 1993 Miss Universe, who is from Russia, is Miss Little Hen (Kouroochkina). She is not little at all, but stands six feet tall. She is from the village of Nick-in-the-Tooth (Cherbinka).

What you'll find here

You will notice different spellings for the word "tzar" throughout this book, such as "czar" and "tsar." It's not that I'm an indifferent speller (although I am), or that we didn't use a proofreader (we did). They are all acceptable and I don't know which is preferred. I wish the Lord of Orthography Books would make up his mind.

Also, whenever I refer to prices in Russia (whether in dollars or in rubles), I use the prices and exchange rates that prevailed while I was in St. Petersburg. There has been massive inflation and massive devaluation of the ruble since then, so the reality today is undoubtedly worse — except for the most powerful bureaucrats (the "nomenklatur") and the most successful criminals (the "red" and "white" mafia).

You will quickly discover there is no plot to this book. There is no real beginning, and definitely no end. So you can pick it up and start reading anywhere you wish. If you want to browse around, go ahead; I won't be offended. You can choose history, geography, politics, romance, adventure, Commie-bashing, liberal-bashing, humor (at least I thought parts were *very* funny), or just nibble at the follies and foibles that make Russians so exasperating, lovable, contemptible, amusing, puzzling, sometimes dangerous, and always interesting.

Much of this book was written as a "stream-of-consciousness." It describes what I thought, felt, and did at the time. Sometimes the "stream" might have gotten clouded by a little too much vodka, or emotion, or even self-doubt. (More than once I found myself muttering, "What in blazes am I *doing* here?") There may even have been times impending malnutrition affected my judgement. (Did *you* ever try to live for months at a time on sausage, potatoes, semi-rotten apples, and shredded carrots? I have some advice for you: Don't.)

As to what the future holds for the nation of Russia or its former satraps, don't expect many answers from me. I don't even know what the future holds for my *own* country, much less Russia.

But I'll be happy to give you my impressions — I'm never shy about that. So join me in a few of the thousand-and-one stories I collected during my own *St. Petersburg Nights*.

I hope some of the mystery, majesty, hope, and beauty of this terribly abused place and tragically abused people impress you as they did me.

William Campbell Douglass, M.D.
Istanbul, Turkey
November 1994

Chapter One

There's No Fool
Like an Old Fool
and Other Wise Proverbs

You don't have to be young to be foolish, although it certainly helps. But one central ingredient to foolishness is love.

Clearly I was in love; and at my age! I was passionately in love with St. Petersburg, Russia — its magnificent architecture and the idealized soul of its people. I felt a passion, a raging, totally unreasonable passion that was utterly beyond my control.

Oh, I wouldn't admit it at the time. I pretended not to be aware of the passion; I saw only the "logical" reasons for moving to St. Petersburg. But the passion was there, and my more in-tune friends could sense it. That was the reason for their confusion. Why on earth would I want to spend a year living in that "Evil Empire"?

A visit made sense, they said. You can see first-hand how bad things are. You can find out in a week what they're doing with photoluminescence. Maybe stay a month. But endure an entire winter there? Suffer the shortages and deprivation that will surely take their toll, and at your age?

They were right. Russia is a dangerous country — particularly if you're over 60. All the rationalization in the world shouldn't have hidden the fact that my quest was more than a little quixotic (some would say idiotic).

But I would hear none of it. Just like the young boy who falls for the older, more experienced woman, the more I was warned of my folly, the more I would proceed. Reason be damned.

It was passion, pure and simple. A love affair with a city I first saw in 1965. Back then she was dark, gray, ugly, and stooped under the weight of communism. But even under her slave name, Leningrad, she was still glorious, because of her awesome architecture.

And so were the Russian people. The few I met — it was a crime to associate with an American back then — were full of fire and cynicism, two of my favorite traits. Communism had taken everything from these people — their right to speak, their right to worship, in some cases even their ability to think. But a fire still burned brightly in many of them, and I was warmed by it.

The Russian people I knew weren't believers in the party or the system. They realized that communism was another evil, in a long list of evils, that had befallen them. These men and women had been captured by a devil, but underneath their surface complacency was a rock-hard determination ... and a boatload of cynicism.

More misfortune would certainly come: that seemed to be the fate of this enormous country. But you could see that no matter what happened — be it Hitler's storm troopers, Stalin's assassination squads, Khrushchev's brutality, or Chernobyl's mushroom cloud — these Russians would endure and survive.

When I first saw it, 30 long years ago, Leningrad was a reflection of these people. Next to the cheap, "utilitarian" housing projects stood the beauty of Russia's past. The minarets of long unused Russian churches remained, faded and filthy, but standing nonetheless. They were like the Russian people — bent, but not broken; looted, but definitely not lifeless.

It was this puzzle, this mixture of East and West, of communism and the czar, that first aroused a passion in me three decades ago. The very fact that I could not consummate my passion, could not be a part of this city and her people, made the passion grow. It smoldered for nearly 30 years and required just the tiniest of breezes for it to blaze anew.

From the first day freedom took its tentative steps in Mother Russia, my mind began to fixate on St. Petersburg, the aging beauty, and the plight of the Russian people.

The object of my affection

There's no fool like an old fool; I know that. But in the course of being foolish we often rise above ourselves. I'm past romanticizing now; my Russian loves burned that out of me. But it's not far from wrong to say that my year-long affair, foolish as it was, was the remedy I needed to cure a growing discontent within me.

I did get to know the object of my desire: the enigmatic St. Petersburg. I saw her in all of her beauty and came face to face with all of her contradictions. I would meet the soul of the Russian people (and come to know the soul of one in particular).

Many times my lover, the city on the Neva, would thrill and disappoint me. How could she not — reality can't match 30 years of idealized dreams. Like so many young lovers, I would go from innocence to experience. What was lost was more than compensated by what was gained. Yet something valuable *was* lost, and I suspect it will never be replaced.

The Russian people remain cynical and they will endure. But seven decades of communist terror have worn away almost all of their resistance. The fire still burns in many Russians. But in countless others the flame has been extinguished and will never return.

We know that animals in captivity loose their ability to hunt, to feed themselves, sometimes even to care. Russia has proven that living for 75 years as a ward of the state can do much the same to a people.

A great deal of my innocent love for Russia and her people was left behind during my first St. Petersburg winter. There are contradictions in these people that most Westerners will never know. The Russians themselves don't understand what drives them; consequently they're often at the mercy of emotions which they don't begin to fathom. Many times they won't even acknowledge their existence.

And like a woman with a checkered past, there's too much history for the country and its people to surmount. We Americans are always confident that the past can be overcome. We're always ready to reinvent ourselves. The past to us is no obstacle.

Europeans know that history can be extremely weighty. It's hard to deny 1,000 years of history — take a look at Bosnia, for renewed confirmation of this fact. But until my Russian experience, I never knew the weight of the past to be so oppressive.

My respect and admiration for those Russians struggling to bring their country into the 20th century has grown with experience. It pains me to think that these efforts may not succeed. I'm no prophet, and I pray I'm wrong, but I fear the worst.

There's a fine line, they say, between love and hatred. I was never a great believer in that axiom, but I'm beginning to understand it. My passion for St. Petersburg burned hot, and like all hot fires, it burned quickly. Now, I can see her in a much clearer light. Now, I'm content to admire her from a distance.

One other lesson I learned: It's been said that love conquers all. To my eternal regret, the poets are wrong.

Chapter Two

Hello My Love,
Goodbye My Lovely

My first St. Petersburg night was spent on a filthy train, sleeping in a cold compartment with three strangers who were probably smugglers. This was a dangerous time, with thieves everywhere and tourists a major target. It was rare for an American to be traveling alone on a Russian train. I was asking for it. They would think nothing of cutting off your finger for a gold ring, worth a year's pay. I hadn't been told about that.

I couldn't sleep. The linen was damp and smelled of chemicals. The train lurched and screeched on turns, vodka fumes from the snoring passengers permeated the air. I kept my hands securely around my dinge. ("Dinge" is the Russian word for money.)

There was a full Russian moon keeping pace with the rattling contraption that was taking me to I knew not what. As I looked at the moon, slipping from cloud to cloud, staying perfectly fixed in the frame of the ice-encrusted, dirty window, I had one of those what-in-the-hell-am-I-doing-here spells, one of many to come during my first few months of loneliness in St. Petersburg.

Let me back up a moment and explain how I happened to be on that midnight train to Russia. It's amazing how your life changes according to the people you meet — sometimes for the better, sometimes not.

In the Spring of 1992, I was in Riga, Latvia, helping set up a phototherapy clinic, when the conversation turned to the state of Russian medicine. My colleague, Uris, a gastroenterologist, said the Russians were doing a lot of work on light therapy, especially in St. Petersburg. I was intrigued — even though I would rather have been with his beautiful stepdaughter. (She was a classic leggy-blonde who seemed to like me. But she was engaged. Isn't that the way it always is?)

I asked, expecting a negative response, if I could pop up there and visit his friends for a few days. "Sure," he replied. "You can go up one night, stay all day, and come back the next night on the late train."

I was astounded. Go to communist Russia tomorrow without a visa? But it was as easy to do as he said. This was just after the "liberation" of the Baltic states and, in the minds of Russian border guards and customs officials, there was no border; it was still one country. I traveled from Latvia to Russia on the night train, both ways, without ever being asked to show a passport.

All of this was a smuggler's paradise, only I didn't know it. Later, after the border became a real border — two hours to get through Russian customs, 15 minutes for the Latvian — I realized I could have made a tidy fortune taking out antique Russian icons. Who knows, except for bad timing (and a merciless conscious) I might have become a rich and successful "importer."

But, on the positive side, my timing was perfect. For at the Moskva railway station, I was met by my great friend-to-be, Dr. Nikolai Chaika and his wife, Galia (also an M.D.). As I mentioned earlier, "Chaika" means "seagull" in Russian, and I would come to refer to him, with love and affection, as Jonathan Livingston Seagull.

A seagull with character

Nikolai Chaika looks like a Russian version of Woody Allen, and he has a morose sense of humor to match. He is the Chief Information Officer at the Pasteur Institute in St. Petersburg. As such, he is responsible for keeping Russian doctors informed on the world literature concerning infectious diseases — sort of a one-man Centers for Disease Control.

Next to Aleksandr Solzhenitsyn and me, Nikolai is the most unsuitable man for the communist/socialist system I have ever met. He simply despises the system, and the system, in turn, despises him. I don't know how he has managed to stay alive and out of the gulag for so long. He does everything wrong — that is, right to you and me, but wrong to his socialist bosses. Nikolai works long hours; he takes his work seriously; he has innovative ideas (which are constantly rejected by the stiff party bureaucrats). He just doesn't play the game, and he won't pretend something is right if it isn't.

With Nikolai in command there would have been no Chernobyl.

This brilliant man has paid the price for his integrity. For 20 years he was forbidden to leave the country for medical meetings. Early in their marriage, Nikolai and Galia were separated for a year, supposedly because their talents were needed in separate places. When they protested, they were told, "It will test your love for each other."

The more he hates the system, the more his hatred is returned, and the greater the price he must pay. After 20 years of service at the Pasteur Institute, his "superiors" continue to pile an inhuman amount of work on him. They want to break Chaika, but they never will. He is loyal to the Institute, but the Institute doesn't care a kopek for him. It is very sad ... and very Russian.

Imagine, if you can, a husband and wife, both with medical degrees, one a specialist in dermatology and infectious diseases and the other a pathologist, with a quality of life far below that of a janitor in the United States. Yet, Nikolai and Galia Chaika manage to eke out some happiness in their extremely restricted existence. They flee to the forest at every opportunity, make a fire, and eat roasted sausage (after sufficient smoking it's barely edible — even the wild cats won't eat it); they go to concerts that cost so little they are essentially free; they visit museums; and they talk with friends. Boy, do Russians like to talk!

Their apartment is on the tenth floor of one of the thousands of concrete block monstrosities that clutter the city. The tiny elevator, dark and smelly, lurches upward with strange clicking noises. If you have elevator phobia, not an uncommon neurosis, you would not be happy in Russia. The good news: most of the time most of them don't work.

The dim hallway leading to their apartment is reminiscent of a 19th century mental institution, which is perhaps not entirely inappropriate in a country where lunatics abound. The trouble is, they're driving deserving people, like the Chaika family, crazy too.

Passing through the creaking, triple-locked door into their apartment was like going from Lebanon to Switzerland in one step. It didn't have the quality or style of a modern Western home, but it was clean, orderly, bright, and warm — a haven from the degenerate hell a few steps away.

Their two children, Tolya and Natasha, seem like any American 20-year-olds. And why wouldn't they? Everything they say, do, and probably think is modeled on the American dream. The son, Tolya, is what Lenin would have called a speculator and ordered shot. Tolya studied business administration in college for four years, but now he is getting a *real* education — buying and selling goods on the street. He is an embryonic capitalist, dealing in what we would consider tiny sums — almost child's play — but it's serious business to him and totally different from the nonsense he was taught in college. He is learning capitalism the right way in Russia — on the streets.

Natasha recently graduated with her degree in medicine. As a fledgling doctor, she will make about $10 a month. She has black hair and so doesn't look too out of place with her very dark Cuban husband, Raul. He is a good fellow and, although he knows Russia is no Miami Beach, he is fighting with all his energy and cunning (and some of Nikolai's) to keep from being sent back to Cuba. That tells us something about Castro's island paradise.

Dinner was standard fare, which is all they can afford. There is very seldom meat, except for the abominable Russian sausage. There was salad with peas, salad with "meat" (specks), and salad with beets. All of these "salads" are potato salad, more or less, with plenty of mayonnaise mixed in. There are a lot of bowls of these various dishes put on the table and, to me at least, they all tasted pretty much the same. The coffee is terrible and of unknown pedigree; unless you go to the Hotel Europa, I suggest you stick with the tea when you're in St. Petersburg.

Nikolai's children have never seen asparagus, artichokes, Kiwi fruit, or lobster, except in pictures. They rarely get real chocolate and haven't had cocoa since they were children. It simply disappeared from the market.

The steaks, fresh fish, and fresh chicken are reserved for the nomenklatur and for the fat cats of the Russian mafia. The one exception are the famous Russian "blue birds" — the tough and tasteless chickens offered to the people. They are starved and cyanotic — thus their nickname.

The Chaikas are among the nicest people you could ever hope to meet — they are working, loving, doing their best. They deserve so much more than they will probably ever have. I will always be grateful to my guardian seagulls.

Welcome to St. Petersburg!

Nikolai and his beloved Galia stood grinning as I disembarked from the pride of the October Railroad. I learned later that they were grinning because they had been so relieved to find me unharmed, with no fingers missing and dinge intact.

I was in a semi-stupor from the voyage of the night before and remember little of the agonizing tour by bus and subway they so eagerly dragged me through that day. It seemed only an instant later that I was back on the October Railroad for another ordeal through the land mines of Russian criminality. I had learned only two things: Russia was different, very different; and I had made two sweet, sensitive, generous, and lifetime friends who would protect me at all costs if I made the insane decision to return to St. Petersburg to live.

On the trip back to Riga, my second St. Petersburg night was a little kinder; or maybe I was just getting used to it. The moon was still there. It reversed direction and again raced with me back to a shabby but safer haven in Latvia.

I had made up my mind, looking at that moon, that the world *is* connected. Russia may be an alien, incomprehensible land, filled with much suffering and populated with sometimes hostile people who can't conceive of the riches we Americans have. But I was convinced the St. Petersburg nights would be kind to me — especially since I had the protection of Jonathan Livingston Seagull and his Galia.

After that first visit, the idea of moving to St. Petersburg began to take on a life of its own. In spite of the concern of my friends and the opposition of my children, I decided that, *yes!*, I would do it. I would take my passion, my anger, and my medicine to Russia.

I flew back to Russia in May for a week and stayed at a Western-type hotel. I found a two-room apartment in the industrial area which Nikolai strongly disapproved of. He had many good reasons — all of which I cheerfully ignored.

It was a dangerous neighborhood; there was no security, and since the apartment was on the first floor, all of the drunks in the building would go past my door at least twice a day. The building was more than a kilometer away from the subway station, so without doubt, Nikolai grimly predicted, I would be mugged some cold St. Petersburg night. On the plus side, my rent was $100 a month. I grabbed at the bargain.

I returned to the North Georgia mountains and packed this and stored that. Six weeks later I headed for my hoped-for Shangri-la on the Neva River.

A tortuous beginning

I flew back to St. Petersburg from New York via Frankfurt, Germany, on a practically empty Delta plane. I stretched out across three seats and had a nice nap, not realizing that it was the last decent rest I would get for a month.

We landed in St. Petersburg in the rain. The arrival terminal was built around the turn of the century. Although it serves a city with a population of five million, it is smaller than the terminal in Aspen, Colorado.

Passport control is located just inside the creaking-door entrance, so all of the passengers had to stand outside in the rain while the indifferent passport inspector carefully browsed through each rich tourist's passport, looking for nothing in particular, but enjoying the trip to far-away places that he would never experience himself. I learned later he makes about $8 a month. He was clearly overpaid.

Once through passport control, we faced total chaos. The luggage came in on a carousel so small that the contents of the average Volkswagen "Bug" would overwhelm it. Suitcases and garment bags spilled out onto the floor in a great heap. There was not even enough room to walk between the piles of luggage while you searched for your bags.

The problem was finally resolved by a couple of burly Russians who yelled out the names on the bags and then, when we replied, tossed them toward the wet and exhausted passengers. I shudder to imagine what it would have been like if the plane had been full.

And then customs: it's the only place I know where they X-ray your bags *after* you have completed your flight, and then open them for inspection. I don't think the X-ray works, but it's an impressive show of security. My two-foot metal cattle prod and a gas pistol went completely unnoticed.

Lost in St. Petersburg

I started the first day of my new life with a mistake. By arriving on Sunday I had insured that nothing would be open — no food, no money exchange, no telephone. Nothing.

Nikolai had written my address down on a piece of paper, so that I could take a taxi from Pulkavo Airport to my apartment. I had the taxi wait until I had unloaded my baggage and then instructed him to take me to the one oasis of incredible luxury I was familiar with in St. Petersburg — the incomparable Grand Hotel Europe, which is just off Nevsky Prospekt near the Russian Museum. I felt I had to break in to my new life gradually — the foul smells, the desolation of the rusting and collapsing two-story factory across from my front window, the yard of weeds, the general sense of a dead society evident all around me — all that could wait until tomorrow; I needed the sights, smells, and sounds of civilization. The Grand Hotel Europe, I knew, was just the place.

I had a four-dollar beer — civilization comes at a high price in Russia — wandered around the elegant marble foyer, and drank in the clean, European wonderfulness of it all. I conversed with my friend Igor, the doorman whom I had met on my previous trip. (Always make friends with the doormen; they know everything and can assist you in a thousand different ways.)

I asked Igor about Lena, the gorgeous blonde who worked at the reception desk and with whom I was totally smitten. She was, he reported, still seeing the hated Michael, who was a bouncer at the restaurant down the street.

Having gotten my ration of the good (not to mention, clean) life, I took the subway back to my apartment. I followed the instructions Nikolai had carefully given me: down the escalator (which runs twice as fast as Western escalators — the only thing in Russia that does), turn right, and take the train that comes on the right side. It sounded simple.

I took the train, endured the open stares of the motley-dressed passengers (Did I have two heads? Was my fly open?), and got off at the third stop as instructed. And I promptly panicked.

THIS WAS NOT MY SLEAZY NEIGHBORHOOD — IT LOOKED WORSE.

My imagination ran wild. There I was, lost in a city of five million people, all of whom knew I was rich beyond their imagination, half of whom couldn't wait to rob and kill me.

After a few more mistakes, I managed to get back to Nevsky Prospekt and my beloved Hotel Europe. I explained my problem to Igor and he asked the logical question: "Well, Doctor, what is your address?"

"I have it written down on a piece of paper," I replied sheepishly, "which is on the dresser in my apartment." I didn't cry, but I felt like it.

"Hmm, that *is* a problem. Well, now, explain to me exactly what your friend, Dr. Chaika, told you to do for the subway journey." Igor is about six feet, six inches tall and he looked down at me like a benevolent giant. His top hat took him up to an even seven feet.

I explained the right-right business and how it had not delivered me home. His eyes widened: "A-hah," he said. I clutched his waistcoat in anticipation. "I have it," he exclaimed. I let go of his waistcoat and dropped to the carpet.

"Yes, yes — tell me," I pleaded.

"Well, it's quite simple. You have to go right, right, AND THEN RIGHT AGAIN. If you had gone to the end of the hall, you would have found another hall and THERE you would turn right and take the train on the right!"

Of course — that was it. I gratefully kissed his hand, hugged him around the knees, threw a 10,000-ruble tip in his direction, and dashed for the subway. I went right, right, and right again; got on the train on the right, got off in three stops and, *horoshow!*, I was back in my very own trash-bin neighborhood.

There was the dead factory, the yawning, Stalinesque entryway to the inner courtyard, the weeds, the dumpster overflowing with rotten garbage. I eagerly entered the dark foyer of my apartment building with its smell of human excrement and cat urine. What a relief — home at last!

Devoured at night

I was "home," but the moon had deserted me behind a shroud of St. Petersburg fog. My protective seagull didn't even know I was in Russia. I didn't want to bother him on the weekend. That was my second mistake. Using my wits and a lot of dumb luck, I told myself I would manage to find the Pasteur Institute on Monday. In the meantime I'd been told that American dollars can get you anything in Russia — including a warm, friendly face and/or a bash on the head. I hoped for the former.

The mosquitos were fierce that first night. There were no screens on the windows of my apartment and wet garbage was piled just a few feet away. What are these winged beasts carrying? Malaria? Yellow fever? Dengue fever? God knows! I poured myself a glass of vodka.

The smell of urine was a constant reminder that this wasn't North Georgia. I had another vodka. Luckily, after a while your nose starts ignoring the smell. I had a third vodka (or was it my fourth, or fifth?) and finally I was able to sleep.

I awoke in the morning after my first night in my new home and looked at myself in the broken and clouded mirror in the bathroom. There were huge bags under my murky eyes. I had drunk too much vodka. I rarely drink excessively, not out of moral conviction, but from purely scientific, medical reasoning: I can't stand hangovers, or the terrible beating my liver gives me the next morning for overloading it with ethanol.

I asked myself: "Why are you here in this squalid trash-bin of a place when you could be living anywhere in the world you wanted?"

I didn't answer. I counted the mosquito bites on my face and neck: six. I checked the hair line: It seemed the same, but how do you know if you lost four, five, or fifty hairs because of a damned fool thing? Once you kill those follicles (not that I know for a fact drinking kills hair follicles, but it seems logical), they never come back. On top of a hangover, I felt guilt.

The self-flagellation over, I returned to the question of the day — why was I here? I'm not usually a list-maker, but in this case it seemed a good way to organize my thoughts and explain to myself why I was in this half-starved, moribund socialist wreck of a place. Here's what I came up with:

1. I have always thought that travel stimulates the mind and keeps you young — maybe the bags under my eyes would go away.

2. The Russian women were beautiful — maybe I would fall in love.

3. I was here for scientific investigation of light therapy — that should be reason enough.

That done, I washed my face and went back to bed.

Chapter Three

Adjusting to
My Crazy New World

The next morning I flashed my magic dollars on the street and brought a car to a screeching stop. Knowing the driver wouldn't understand English, I said the only thing he would possibly understand, "Hotel Europe."

He grinned and replied, "Da, spaceeba, horoshow," and away we went. I endured a continual babble of Russian all the way down Nevsky Prospekt. The only word I understood was "Americanze." I smiled and nodded my head; we got along just fine.

I no doubt paid him several times the regular fare, but who cares? He delivered me to an oasis of English when he could have taken me to some Kafkaesk dark courtyard and had my guts torn out — to say nothing of my dinge.

Earlier that Sunday morning I'd gotten a lesson in the drunken anarchy that is so common in Russia. I was walking along a street lined with kiosks selling the usual vodka, beer, and cigarettes. A few paces in front of me, a drunken Russian was weaving along the sidewalk with an unopened bottle of beer in each hand. He put the two bottle caps together to pull one off with the other. He turned the opened bottle up and emptied it in less than a minute. Then he tossed it against the side of a building, where it exploded and scattered glass for yards around.

The other pedestrians pretended not to notice. The drunk staggered his way around the corner.

I would witness this sort of psychotic behavior almost every day during my year in St. Petersburg, but I never got used to it. It must be a result of genetic downgrading through mass murder, combined with despair and hopelessness. Many of the intelligent people left in Russia (yes, there are some) feel nothing can be done within their country to save it. Russia, they will tell you, needs to be conquered by a superior civili-zation. The Russian people need someone to tell them what to do. That seemed terribly drastic to me and was a sad commentary on a nation that only 70 years ago was headed for greatness. I, being new on the block, reserved judgment.

Many times during the muggy July and August nights the what-in-the-hell-am-I-doing-here feeling returned. There was a weedy park alongside the Neva, only a few blocks from my Stalinesque concrete prison. Nikolai warned me to stay away from the park — it was simply too dangerous. But I had to get away, if only to escape the mosquitos, which were worse inside than out.

I carried my stun gun for protection. Poverty and a crushing communist state can drive even the most honest people to a life of crime. Plus, the new Russia had developed a powerful, threatening underworld where anything goes and the price of life is cheaper than the ruble.

I quickly found out that crime in Russia is one — perhaps the only — growth industry. It's not just the Russian mafia, powerful as that underground army is; crime has become a national pastime, perhaps the country's most popular cottage industry. The highwaymen of old have returned. Like the gangs in our Wild West, their favorite targets are trains.

Entire villages will participate in attacking a train. The tracks will be blown up, stopping the train, which is then assaulted by young and old. Everything is stripped, including the passengers.

According to the Russian press, there were 11,000 train ambushes in the first three months of 1993 alone. Yes, I know Russia is a huge country; but think of that number — eleven *thousand* train robberies in just three months! Some trains are now carrying guards armed with automatic weapons and — I kid you not — even rocket launchers, for protection when they are attacked with stolen armored military vehicles.

War is hell, especially when you have to shoot old women in babushkas and children attacking a train wild-west style. Maybe there's a black comedy here somewhere: Shoot-Out at the OK Kabak, Blazing Babushkas; something like that.

Back to my stroll around my desolate patch of St. Petersburg. The truth was, I was so bored and lonely I would almost have welcomed an attack, but no such luck. Drunks would amble by and mutter something incomprehensible. I'd reply, "Ya nea gavaru pa Ruskie," which was as close as I could come to saying, "I don't speak Russian." They would laugh at my accent and stagger off.

Companionship and coffee

The park was almost, but not quite, as depressing as my apartment. The Neva River bordered the park for more than a kilometer, but the entire river view was blocked by a line of rusting garbage dumpsters. As Yakov Smirnoff would say, What a country!

My imagination sometimes worked overtime. You have no idea what the people are saying; at any minute you expect an ax to come through the door of your flat and hear a mob shouting, "GET THE RICH AMERICAN!"

And your mind starts wondering: What would I do if I suddenly became ill? The answer was simple — I would die. No air evac, just a quick trip to one of those mortuaries called a Russian hospital.

I maintained what was left of my sanity by dreaming of past loves. Or the stunning, intelligent, sensitive, deeply understanding Russian woman I would soon meet. Still unnamed, she would have brilliant white teeth (I was being picky; that's not easy to find in Russia). We would live happily ever after, locked in each other's arms, far from St. Petersburg. Was there such a creature waiting for me amongst the great unwashed of St. Petersburg? Out of 5 million people there must be one — preferably about age 29.

As you can see, it's easy to go a little crazy in Mother Russia. But there was an oasis to assuage my incipient psychosis — the fabulous, elegant, efficient, clean, courteous Grand Hotel Europe — and its pretty assistant manager, Rose Marie, a gorgeous Swedish redhead.

At that time, desperate for company — looking for recognition that I did actually exist; that *this place*, and not me, was screwed up — having the opportunity to speak English without stumbling, halting, or hesitation was wonderful. To use the subtleties of the language and to know that they are understood and appreciated by an attractive woman was just what the doctor ordered. Rose Marie was a great therapy for me.

Her English was flawless and in those early days of disorientation and insecurity, she became my psychiatrist, although she didn't know it. But, then again, maybe she did. Women are more perceptive than men and easily see through our pretenses.

Rose Marie had dark red-brown hair, pale blue eyes, light skin, and just a trace of freckles. I could have fallen in love with her if she had been interested, but she only liked me "as a person," if you know what I mean.

She was always busy and carried a beeper. Our visits were never for more than 30 minutes. She'd join me for coffee on the second-floor mezzanine. It was the only place in town where you could get a decent cup of Western-style brew. Her beeper would go off 29 minutes later. I figured she planned it that way. I used to do the same thing to get away from a patient who was too involved with himself, so that was okay; I understood.

Rose Marie reminded me of the typical American career woman — efficient, hard-working, ambitious, and bound to succeed. But I couldn't help but wonder about the other woman inside her. I hope she falls in love with a Swedish prince and has five beautiful children. I think that's what she really wants, but I could be wrong. When it comes to women, I often am.

The Russian people are a curious dichotomy of strengths and weaknesses. They have endured much, and continue to endure terrible indignities from the state apparatus. Grandparents stand in long lines every month at the post office in all kinds of weather, including 40 degrees below zero, to collect their tiny pensions. These are delivered as a stack of almost worthless coins.

If the window slams down at 6:00 pm, and you have waited in line for eight hours, you will have to come back tomorrow and start all over again. When you get to the cash window the next day, you will be asked, "Why weren't you here yesterday — you were supposed to be here YESTERDAY." If you're unlucky, they won't accept your explanation — their bureaucrats can be unbelievably petty and nasty — and you will lose your pension for that month.

One time, before we left on a three-day trip to Novgorod, Nikolai made arrangements for the office in charge of passports to clear my visa, so I could leave for Helsinki on our return. The proper documents were left with the officials. It was supposedly a routine matter — what they were paid to do.

When we returned, the doctor-bureaucrats had done nothing. There had been a holiday, they needed my signature, etc., etc. Nikolai's eyes bulged and his face turned purple: "Why didn't you sign it yourself? Nobody cares as long as your precious seal is there. Can't you think for yourself once in a while?" Nose to nose they stood — two doctors going at it like Russian bears in a torrent of Cyrillic invective.

Later I asked another doctor why nothing had been done about my passport. She simply shrugged. "This is Russia," was her sardonic reply..

Nikolai moves me uptown

Nikolai insisted that I move out of my flat-on-the-Neva at Dumpster Row, and when a seagull makes up his mind there's no going back. I think he knew I was losing it. Maybe the fact that I had lost 15 pounds in two weeks was a giveaway. "Do you have AIDS, Beel?" was his clever way of putting it.

This time I let him choose my quarters and, as always, he came through with the perfect place for a lonely, fish-out-of-water American. It was on Kaminostrovoski Prospekt next to a lovely, weedless park. It was two blocks away from the Neva River, and no dumpsters were in sight. Best of all there were actually some happy-looking people around, including a few attractive women. Maybe my loneliness would disappear; maybe I would learn to like the place. Maybe I would find my Russian princess and fall in love.

Nikolai and Galia stocked my refrigerator, so I finally had something to eat. By the beginning of October, the mosquitos and flies had left. I had a CD player and an ample supply of American music, including my beloved Errol Garner. Home, sweet home!

On the inside, the new apartment was little different from my first one. Almost all apartments in Russian flats look alike. It's like walking into a black-and-white version of Blanche's apartment in "A Streetcar Named Desire." An amusing aside about socialist furniture: The cushions for the back of the divans are the exact same dimension as those for the seat. If you push the seat squares under the back ones, they are too short and the inside of your knees hit the couch frame. But if you push the back squares down behind the seats, the seat squares hang over the front edge and the back cushions don't come up high enough.

Maybe different factories make the backs and bottoms and they have never been able to get together. Maybe the human model they used 50 years ago was short and squatty. Maybe they just don't care! I'm not sure what the explanation is, but what amazed me the most was that no one else seemed to notice.

As in the other apartment, there were no screens in the windows. I don't know how they stand the mosquitoes. I asked Nikolai about this and received his usual sardonic reply: "In building socialism, Beel, you must put up with these little inconveniences."

Getting my own telephone

The owners of my new flat guaranteed me a telephone would be installed "right away." The telephone was one reason I was willing to pay the outrageous rent of $250 a month — two-and-a-half times the previous rate.

Two weeks later, a device that looked like it came from a 1940s toy store was installed. What they hadn't bothered to explain to me was that the contraption was a bootleg deal. They had hooked in to my neighbor's phone; I was to pay him a small fee for sharing our home-made party line.

A new hookup, they explained, would cost $500 and take six months to get installed — if you were lucky. Not willing to wait, I agreed to the arrangement.

I felt a sense of panic: how would I communicate with my Atlanta office with such a primitive contraption? How would the neighbors, a Russian engineer and his family, none of whom had ever left the country, explain to the authorities telephone calls to and from every corner of the globe? Would we all be arrested as CIA agents? Would I be allowed to read in jail? Did they serve coffee in jail? Did they have *mosquitoes* in jail?

At first the system was a disaster. Whenever I answered the phone, it would be a person speaking Russian; I would hang up. Whenever my neighbors answered and it was someone speaking English, *they* would hang up. I offered a simple solution to the problem: Install a buzzer from their flat to mine. I would not answer the phone and, in fact, would turn my bell off. So if someone called in English, just buzz me.

To the surprise of both of us, the new arrangement worked. That is, it worked partly. My buzzer went off; I picked up the phone: "Hello, Bill? How are you? It's great to finally talk with..." Click — buzz, buzz. A conversation from the U.S. seldom lasted more than a minute.

Making a call was even worse. It might take 15 or 20 attempts before my outgoing calls made it past the Russian border. And the worst part of it was — just give me a few more minutes and I'll get off this ridiculous subject; you're the only person I can talk to — I got charged *every time* I attempted to make a call to the outside world. If it took 20 attempts for a call to go through, I got charged for 20 international calls! I had to pay for *their* mistakes.

I didn't discover this until I got my first bill which, of course, came to my neighbor's apartment. It almost gave him a heart attack. It was for a little over $500. When they saw it, his entire family panicked.

He makes $15 a month, so I can guess what they thought. The bill represented *two-and-a-half **years*** of his pay. I'm sure it looked like $50,000 to him. Surely I wouldn't be able to pay it. What if I died, or skipped out, or got arrested? What if I got *both* of us arrested?

When he knocked on my door, he was breathing hard and looked close to apoplexy. His wife was behind him, crying and moaning. His daughter, who had always smiled at me, was grim-faced. This $500 bill was a potential disaster beyond an American's understanding. It would take him the rest of his life to pay it off. Then there was the spy thing. At the very least, he would certainly lose his precious telephone. At the worst ... well, it didn't bear thinking about.

I had Nikolai take me to the telephone office first thing the next morning. After waiting in line for only an hour and a half — it was a slow day — we paid the bill. I gave Petr the receipt and he responded as though he had won the state lottery. His wife quit sniveling and his daughter started smiling at me again. She said she wanted to teach me Russian — hmm, dazzled by that $500 payment, I suspect. She's a math major at St. Petersburg U., but you don't have to be a whiz at math to know I was a billionaire in their eyes.

Realizing that I'd be charged for 15-20 calls for every one that went through, I soon gave up on the telephone. When there was no rush, I sent discs by air mail; it took about two weeks but they usually made it okay. If my publisher was in a hurry, I sent them UPS or DHL. And if there was a real rush for comments or copy, I used the fax at the post office or the Hotel

Europe. They were expensive — but not as costly as a dozen or two international calls that didn't go through.

Safety in numbers

Summer nights in northern Russia can be an exhilarating and unforgettable experience. To put it in modern terms, the sky at 3:00 am looks like the silver glow of a giant, blank computer screen. That may not sound romantic, but under its glow, the city is indeed a romantic place. Now, if only I had someone to share it with.

The young women of Russia look quite fashionable, and they do it with very little money. Most of them have bodies that Western women spend half their lives in the exercise room trying to achieve. A Russian beauty would starve rather than do without her cosmetics. Maybe that's one reason they're so slender.

Not unlike my life back home, my new existence revolved around medical doings and writing my newsletter. Things were better, but something was missing. I can't explain it, but if you've ever lived away from America you know what I mean. No matter how beautiful the architecture and no matter how nice the locals are, something isn't quite right. (A 1905 apartment with 1930s furniture isn't beautiful, but I pretended to enjoy the "atmosphere.")

Ironically, the only serious threat of mayhem to my body came after I moved from the dangerous industrial area to the relatively safe Petrogradskyia region. I was well settled in to my new apartment and, for the first time, I really felt like Dr. Zhivago. I was ambling through the neighborhood of the decaying, late-19th century buildings on a particularly beautiful early fall day. I was enjoying the crisp St. Petersburg air and the beautiful autumn leaves. Even the sight of a drunk collapsed at the bottom of a brilliant gold birch tree seemed harmonious, as the leaves swirled around him as if protecting him from the bitter world of which he was a reluctant part.

There I was, a modern Zhivago — brilliant scientist, brave protector of the beautiful Lara (I was impatiently waiting for that part), stalwart participant in the great Russian struggle for freedom and democracy, or something like that.

I was walking along a narrow park between some apartments when my usual Dr. Zhivago fantasy was interrupted by calls in Russian from three men behind me. They were wearing imitation black-leather jackets, the typical uniform of Cacusian thugs. They were about 50 yards back, black-haired, swarthy, and obviously dangerous. To them I was easy pickings — a leather-covered money bag with a valuable passport.

I had become complacent and had left my cattle prod and gas gun in the apartment. Their calls became more strident as they started to close in on me. I quickened my pace ever so slightly, not wanting to provoke them into a dog-pack rush.

I turned the corner toward the subway station, knowing they would not attack in a crowded place. A mob of people poured out of a bus, slowing my would-be robbers for a moment and giving me that extra step I needed to make it to the subway station. I ran up the stairs, knowing I had beaten them; I had a monthly subway pass which I could flash and dash down the escalator while they fumbled for coins.

I was safe, if out of breath and with a heart rate over 200. I went to the Hotel Europe and ordered a double Scotch.

I never went out without my stun gun and gas pistol again. I continued to wear my hats, usually my confederate cavalry officer's grey with the gold cord around the base. I suppose it was foolish, naive, and perhaps a little vain for an obvious foreigner to walk around St. Petersburg alone at any time of day or night. But this was the only time I was threatened while walking the byways of the city. God and the spirit of Robert E. Lee must have been looking over me.

Speaking of vanity, I have a theory: anybody my age can look like an old geezer. But if you want to look like *a real cantankerous coot from Hades*, you've got to wear a hat.

Besides, it gives me something to tip to the ladies.

Chapter Four

Standard of Living?
What Standard of Living?

On February 23, 1988, at 6:20 in the afternoon, a shot was fired from the famous cannon at the Peter and Paul Fortress. It was to celebrate the birth of Pavlic Rusakov, St. Petersburg's five millionth citizen.

It's been straight downhill for the city since the welcoming of little Pavlic. The population now stands at 4,960,000 and continues to fall. The only things not falling are the price of food and the death rate. The price of bread has gone up 63 times in the past seven years; the price of sugar 90 times. The people aren't starving, but malnutrition is a severe problem and is getting worse. There were 62,766 recorded deaths in 1991; that was up from 61,541 in 1990.

The Russian birth rate is one of the lowest in the world. It's sad that these beautiful people aren't reproducing themselves. Instead, they've turned to animal worship — their pets. Many Americans are doing the same thing, but at least the Russians have a good excuse.

The statistics on the deterioration of the population are appalling: The birth rate has fallen since the birth of little Pavlic from 16 per 1000 to 10.6 per 1000. The death rate has increased from 10.7 per 1000 to 12. And these are *official* figures from the State Committee of Statistics. The real story is probably worse.

With a recent poll showing that only four percent of the people had faith in the government's ability to solve Russia's problems, bringing children into this world is not an attractive prospect to the average Russian couple.

The reluctance about having children goes to startling extremes: A lot of children are abandoned to the state. The form reads in part: "I hereby permanently relinquish custody of my child. I commit his life to state institutions...." There are over 5,000 orphans in St. Petersburg alone. But here's the real shocker: Only three percent of them are actually orphans; the rest of them are children whose parents abandoned them. Many of the kindergarten-aged children can't walk, speak, or use a spoon. Most of them have multiple diseases.

At Orphanage Number Four, the staff works valiantly to help these pathetic little creatures. They are taught to grow flowers and vegetables and they take care of hens. Following the precepts of Russian folk medicine, they are given a cold bath every morning, summer and winter.

Lena K., age six, is in a constant state of excitement. She has been adopted and will soon leave for Canada. She carries a picture of her new parents everywhere and is always asking someone to reread their letters to her. She hears a car and rushes to the window, crying, "Maybe they've come for me."

They have a room at Number Four, called the "psychological relief room," where the children can do anything they want, including tearing it completely to pieces, without being punished. The director, Raisa Ratner, says, "Our aim is to heal the children's hearts." God bless you, Raisa.

Fido, the family favorite

You will find this hard to believe, but in Russia the family member who is valued more highly than children is ... the dog. I have never seen a country, including our own, where the family pet is as cherished, cosseted, and protected as it is here. Food may be scarce, but the dog will get his share.

Most of these pets, in this extremely poor country, are costly thoroughbreds. Russians will have expensive professional portraits made of themselves with their dog. They will shower as much or more attention on a baby puppy as they would a human baby, even to the point of wrapping their "foundling" in a blanket and carrying it around with them. In the cold winter months, some of the dogs are better dressed than the people.

Children get little attention. The people "ooh" and "ahh" over puppies, but not over babies. Half the men are alcoholics who have deserted their families, leaving the women to work and support their children at near-starvation wages. Russian mothers seem to have little time for love. They don't walk with their children — they drag them along beside them. The child has to trot to keep up.

The saddest and most depressing statistic in these hard times is the one concerning infant murders — 2,000 infants were killed by their parents in Russia in the past five years. And those are just the *reported* deaths; the real number is undoubtedly many times higher. In addition, another 2,000 children take their own lives each year.

These grim figures coincide with other newspaper reports about parental abuse. If they could, many Russian parents would sell their children into slavery. One young couple came close to it — they advertised to trade their child for a large apartment.

I wouldn't be surprised to see a dog in a baby carriage with a child trotting along behind, attached to a leash around the neck. After all, dogs and cats are referred to as persons (kto), not common things (chto.) It seems to me an appropriate greeting in Russia would be: "Hello, how's your dog?" I can assure you they wouldn't trade their beloved dog for an apartment. He's FAMILY.

Even the cruelest of commissars will show this sentimental adoration of pets. There was a stern and brutish general, feared by all because of his total disregard for the lives of colleagues and enemies alike, who had a pet parrot that was carried with him everywhere. When the parrot died, he cried like a heart-broken child.

Beautiful pessimists

Working-age Russians have their own set of problems — not as desperate as the problems of the young and old, but almost as psychologically and morally debilitating. Privacy is almost impossible to find. You can't do more than hold hands with your girlfriend in the average flat, because there will be half-a-dozen or more other people living there, from newborns to aunts, uncles, and grandparents.

Courting with a modicum of privacy is only possible at the local parks. But how romantic can you be there, when it's 30 degrees *below* freezing? Can you understand why many Russians don't want children and shower what little affection they can muster on dogs?

In the good old days, when sex was supposed to be for producing new members for the Young Communist League and nothing else, everything was simple: Husbands loved their wives; wives loved their husbands; and the state loved everybody. When I was in Russia in 1965, I was struck by the lack of beautiful women. On returning in 1992, I realized they had only been in hiding. Back then, it wasn't patriotic to look feminine and alluring; you had to look like you could wield a 40-pound hammer with one hand and strangle a German with the other.

Boy, have things changed. Now, not a day goes by that I don't see at least three Marilyn Monroes, one Jaclyn Smith, and a Michelle Pfeiffer or two. There are Kelly LeBrocks and Anne Archers, too.

Russia is now experiencing a veritable epidemic of post-communist lust for the "good life." Many of her citizens are willing to pay almost any price for it. The classifieds, as in any country, tell it all. Many of the women will sell their body, or at least rent some part thereof: "I am willing to give birth to a baby for a childless couple. I am 36, beautiful and healthy. Price negotiable."

The beefy broad in the babushka is no longer the symbol of Russian womanhood. Jack boots and baggy pants are out; high heels and Spandex are in. Many of them say they hate men, but they sure don't dress like it. They've gone from the dark shadows of the socialist state to the hardest of direct sells in one ballerina leap — and minus the tu-tu: "Beautiful young woman offers sexual favors to rich man." Not much romance there, but it's not ambiguous, either. And I got that one from a publication of the Young Communist League!

Don't get the idea that all the young women wear a bar code on their nether parts. There are many strong, moral, intelligent, and beautiful Russian women who are world class in every way. They deserve a little Western spoiling. (I'm doing the best I can, but I need help; I can't do it all myself.)

One is tempted to hypothesize that, after 70 years of brutal oppression, most of the Russian people have given up on humanity, except for raw sex, and have turned their affection to a more trustworthy species — their dog. They don't have the great affection for children that one sees in the U.S., Japan, and, in fact, most countries, whether developed or undeveloped.

"It's not in the budget"

Having dozens of Russian medical associates, I can relate to the pay scale of scientists better than most Westerners. My friend Mike Plouzhnikov is the chief of ear, nose, and throat surgery (otolaryngology) at the best such facility in Russia, the Pavlov Medical Institute. He is also president of the All-Union ENT Scientific Society.

Mike is about 45 years old, full of enthusiasm, and has a non-stop sense of humor. He does laser throat surgery that would be the envy of many Western institutions. He's the only such surgeon in the entire former Soviet Union, and he trains young ENT specialists from all over the world; I met one from Syria and another from the steppes of Mongolia.

Mike makes $20 a month. The night watchman at the Pavlov Medical Institute makes almost twice as much. Think of it: Many of the drunks on the street make more than the most prestigious ENT surgeon in Russia.

Some educated and highly qualified Russians rebel at the system and refuse to give away their talent to a government that only appreciates the common man. Ludmilla is a graduate of St. Petersburg University. For 25 years she worked at the Pasteur Institute, devoting herself to a legal specialty (something to do with patent law) that was unknown in Russia before her work.

Her extraordinary skills and intelligence meant earning a pauper's salary of about $15 a month. She informed her director that she no longer wished to do her patent work and was resigning. He said: "How can you do this? Your work is extremely valuable to us and the state."

"Then why don't you pay me a decent salary for my extremely valuable work?" she retorted.

"We couldn't possibly raise your salary. It's not in the budget," was the reply.

But here's the real kicker: Ludmilla resigned her post and promptly got another job in the very same building, working as a security person at the reception desk — for *twice* her previous salary.

Doctors get only 150 rubles for making a house call in Russia. After he pays his expenses (including 50 rubles to his bureaucratic physician boss), he'll net less than 100 rubles — or about 25 cents.

(It's interesting to note that psychiatrists, while still terribly underpaid by Western standards, will make on the average *twice* what a regular M.D. gets. The commies held psychiatrists in very high regard. From the time of Pavlov, mind manipulation was recognized as an important tool to make the people appreciate the socialist state.)

It is remarkable how many college graduates, often with doctor's degrees, are engaged in menial work in Russia. There's the doctor who peddles trinkets on the streets of Moscow; our patent expert mentioned above; a college-graduate cartographer I met in a park near the Gorky statue who sells his paintings for $5 each (and thereby makes five times his state salary); a graduate nuclear engineer who works as a carpenter.

My young Russian teacher, Oolia, a pretty blonde with the standard Russian-grey eyes, has a degree in linguistic mathematics. (Don't ask me what that means.) Oolia told me that most of her friends, all with at least one college degree, work as waiters and waitresses at the Hotel Europe. I know that my favorite waiter there is a graduate mining engineer.

Many of the women who are beautiful, but brainless, go into prostitution. They can make $300 or more a night — that's a *year's* salary for their parents — and retire at an early age. Well, maybe they're not brainless, just willing to exchange their self-respect and risk their health for a little security. Half the young women in Moscow, one newspaper reported, said they considered prostitution a desirable career.

I was once propositioned by a delectable little creature in front of the Astoria Hotel. I asked her (as research for this book, you understand) what the going rate was. She replied that it was $300. Knowing that was a year's pay for many Russians, I couldn't resist a follow-up question: "Is that per week or per month?"

She tossed her blonde mane contemptuously and swivel-hipped down the sidewalk, knowing she was giving me a good look at what I was missing. And I didn't pay a kopek for the look.

The hope for the future

In spite of my growing negativity, something always happens in St. Petersburg that makes me think things will get better. Tonight was no different.

I returned from my usual evening walk along the Neva River to find a group of six teenagers, four boys and two girls, sitting on the steps inside the large foyer that leads up to my apartment.

It was raining pretty hard, so my steps had become their refuge. They had no other place to go except to their families' apartments, which are always crowded with grumpy, exhausted, and often drunken relatives who are not interested in the kids' music, loves, or hopes, because they themselves have no hope.

Two of the young men were making very nice American music on their guitars ("Michelle, my belle..."). The smaller of the four boys was obviously the court jester and the other one was preoccupied trying to seduce one of the two girls. One girl was shockingly beautiful, a Russian Kathleen Turner and, I think, the girlfriend of one of the two guitar players. She flirted just enough to attract my attention.

I went up to my apartment, then decided to go back to make friends with them. They talked in Russian and I talked in English. We didn't understood each other, but we were enjoying the music and each other's company.

And here is the point to all this, other than the fact that I was smitten by yet another young Russian lovely. I offered to bring down some vodka for them and they said, "no, thank you," they didn't drink.

Imagine that: Russian teetotalers! There is a great soul in this sad country trying to break free.

I hope it succeeds.

Chapter Five

Russia's Terrible History

The first few months in a new country are always difficult. You have to learn how everything is done — how the locals do it, so to speak. Now if you're moving, say, to England, you can ask someone where to shop. The difference between American and English is vast, no doubt, but it *can* be overcome.

In Russia, the problems you'll encounter are compounded by a society that, even in the best of times, has its own ways of doing things — ways that are often nonsensical to the outsider. (Many of them are nonsensical to the average Russian, too.) Of course, you're doubly handicapped by the Russian alphabet — a series of twisting, turning, backward symbols which makes reading even the most basic sign impossible.

Add to this more than 70 years of communist stupidity, the current economic chaos, the vast mixture of races and cultures, and a checkered history which extends through a thousand years and dozens of czars and czarinas, and you have an idea of what must be faced by any American crazy enough to follow my lead.

I was aware of some of the problems. But you can't ever be fully prepared.

During those first few months, when I had a lot of time on my hands and spent most evenings in my darkened apartment, armed only with a bottle of vodka and visions of some Russian beauty I had seen walking the streets of St. Petersburg, I decided to bone up on my Russian history.

I quickly became an armchair aficionado of the Russian royal families, from Ivan the Terrible to the ill-fated Nicholas II. Somewhere in the stories of the czars, the harsh Russian winters, and the ceaseless suffering of the populace, I grew closer to the Russian people.

Their odd ways of doing things, their ideas on family, on government, on work, on life in general, are inextricably linked with their history. Like the stiff-upper-lipped Brits, who watch with a combination of pride and dismay when Chuck and Di battle it out in the tabloids, these Russians are forever bound to their royal families, whether they realize it or not.

The more I read and the more people I met, the more I became convinced that to understand Russia, you must know something of its amazing, brutal history. Not only the history of communism — those years are just a small blip on a thousand-year screen — but the *real* history of Russia, the Russian monarchy.

Ivan the Awesome

If you just can't stand history, skip this section. *But you really should read it. If you don't, you will miss some incredible violence and some awesome sex.*

Ivan the Terrible wasn't really his name. It was Ivan the Awesome — but he *was* terrible. Ivan can claim the title of the greatest wife-abuser of all time. In 1546, at the age of 17, he married Anastasia. After three weeks of marriage, she "died unexpectedly."

The next czarina was Maria, the beautiful "southerner" who was as promiscuous as Ivan. She was said to change lovers on a daily basis. At one time she had a harem of her own consisting of 30 lovers. The czar was informed and said he would "pray to God for her." She soon "fell ill" and died.

Next came Martha. She "grew thin and died" — poisoned by the father of the previous czarina, historians now believe. Anna was Ivan's next bride. He forced her into a monastery where she lived for 54 years. (She was the lucky one.)

Ivan next married another Maria. It was reported to him that she had sex with someone else the night before their wedding. He had her drowned in an ice hole.

Then came another Anna. In three months she "died of a cruel illness."

A czarist official, Nikita Melentyev, had a wife who caught Ivan's fancy. Ivan invited Nikita to the palace to have a glass of wine; poor Nikita never made it home. Two days later, his grieving widow, Vasilisa, moved into the palace. It wasn't long before one of Ivan's aids found her in bed with the czar's falconer. Ivan, always creative, killed the falconer and then put Vasilisa, still alive, into the coffin with him and buried them both.

There were a few other unsuccessful marriages, but one bride, the third Maria, managed to live long enough to bear him a son, Dmitri. But as the saying goes, it's a wise man who knows his father. Some of the other czars were also terrible, but none ever matched Ivan.

Czar Alexander Nevski is much revered and was, in fact, sanctified by the Russian Orthodox Church. He should have been called Alexander the Brown-Nose. In order to save his property and his neck, he served as enforcer for the Mongol horde. But he was a great general; he defeated the Germans in the west and then socked it to the Swedes in the north. So the church overlooked the enforcer bit and he is now Saint Alex.

Perhaps the greatest ruler of Russia was Catherine the Great. She may be best known today for her sexual excesses, but she was as close to a Jeffersonian liberal as Russia would see, at least until the reign of Nicholas II. Many Russians believe that she died during a sexual romp with a horse, when the scaffolding collapsed and her favorite steed crushed her to death. (Like the British, the Russians revel in preposterous stories about their royal betters.)

No one knows if this story is true. Catherine did have her husband, the czar, murdered so she could ascend to the throne, of that there is no doubt.

From the first czar to the last, nothing much changed for the Russian people. There was a small middle class of shopkeepers and tax collectors who were completely subservient to the czar. The vast majority of Russians were serfs who would labor for someone else until they died. Most of the world still works on this schedule; it wasn't unique to civilization then or now.

You have to remember that the czars in Russia owned everything and everybody. It was an oriental version of a southern plantation. Peter the Great needed tens of thousands of workers to build his dream city, St. Petersburg, on the Gulf of Finland. The engineers tried to tell him it wasn't a good idea. In fact, they said, it was the worst possible location for the city, out of many bad possibilities he considered.

But Peter wouldn't listen. So he built the Venice of the North with slave labor from all over the kingdom. Naturally, building a major city on a swamp led to the death of many thousands. But more on that later.

The other side of the story

But there is another side to the rule of the czars. In spite of the bad press the czars have always received, from the reign of Peter the Great in the early 18th century, through the last czar, Nicholas II, there was a steady progression toward freedom and self-government. There was a reversion to severe repression during the reign of Alexander III but, after all, the anarchists killed his father, Alexander the Liberator, who freed the serfs. Can you blame him for being a little testy? As it turned out, his son, Nicholas II, was massacred along with the czarina and their five children, on the direct order of Lenin.

From Peter the Great in the early 1700s to the communist takeover in 1917, the czars, almost without exception, wanted and actually tried to bring constitutional and representative government to their nation. But what do you do when your subjects love an authority figure and want direction from the top and yet, at the same time, have a strong streak of anarchy coursing through their veins? Contrary to what you have been led to believe, the czars weren't the big bad guys (and gals) that they have been depicted. Professor Charles Sarolea of Edinburgh University, an authority on Russian history, got it right when he said:

> The Russian state was not undemocratic — on the contrary if anything, there was too much democracy.... The reason why the popular masses so easily fell prey to the bolshevist tyranny lies mainly in the exaggerated spirit of egalitarianism *supported and encouraged by the monarchy.* [Emphasis added]

For example, when the serfs were freed by Alexander II, the state did not hesitate to endow these free citizens with adequate land holdings from private landowners who had enjoyed government-enforced monopolies. This was an act of social radicalism that no non-revolutionary government in Russia had ever dreamed of introducing.

Our own President Taft, speaking before some prominent Russians in 1912, said: "Your emperor has introduced legislation for the working classes more perfect than that which any of the democratic countries boast."

Alexander II, "The Liberator," even followed the lead of the pre-Civil War United States in upholding the principle of "states' rights." Let me quote from the preamble of the new regulations he promulgated for a free Russia:

> Each Province and District possesses its own individual interests and is faced with local problems. The management of these interests should be entrusted to the Province and District concerned, on lines similar to those which obtain in any private enterprise, directed by a private individual. The owner is the person best suited to direct a business, as it is he who suffers the consequences of mismanagement and bears the burden of responsibility.

I would accept these "regulations" of 1864 over anything our own government has promulgated in the past 130 years. Wouldn't you?

The truth is that there was a rapidly developing and fairly mature free economy in Russia, and a definite movement toward a constitutional republic based on the American model. The Russian people had no quarrel with the monarchy and, in fact, loved it. They would have been very happy with, and were well-suited for, a constitutional monarchy similar to Britain's.

The immense and eventually successful effort of Czar Nicholas II to create a strong, landed middle class has no precedent in history. Between 1894 and the fall of the monarchy in 1917, he turned 100 million acres of land over to peasants in Siberia and moved 5 1/2 million emigrants there.

Ironically, the greatest obstacle to forming a free, independent, land-owning class was Russia's ancient tradition of communal farming, which had been a way of life in the country for hundreds of years.

But Nicholas, ably assisted by one of Russia's greatest statesmen, Petr Stolpin, persisted. Despite the resistance of much of the aristocracy and even a very hostile "liberal" press, they were eventually successful. A strong, independent middle class began to emerge.

The resultant prosperity was stunning. Russia rapidly became a major exporter of goods. By 1913, grain production, for example, was 28 percent greater than the *combined* production of Argentina, Canada, and the United States.

By that year (four years before the Bolshevik revolution), Russia supplied 50 percent of the total world trade in eggs. It was the largest sugar producer on the planet. The same success story also applied to cotton, livestock, butter, and many other items.

In 1913, as America amended our Constitution to accept the second plank of the Communist Manifesto — a heavy graduated income tax — Russia was one of the most tax-free nations on earth. Total taxation, direct and indirect, amounted to less than ten percent a year! By comparison, in Britain it was approaching 40 percent; in France it was over 30 percent. (In the United

States today, it is *over 50 percent* for many professional and business people.)

It is safe to say that in no other country in the world, including the United States, was the general prosperity and well-being of the working masses improving more rapidly than in czarist Russia during the last decade of their reign.

In the 1950s, Khrushchev boasted that Soviet farm production had finally reached the levels of the czarist year 1913. Imagine that: It took the Soviet tractor 40 years to finish in a dead heat with the czarist horse and plow!

But the "liberals" could never forgive Stolpin and the czar for their stupendous success in liberating the Russian people from the chains of socialism and paternalism. They publicly applauded when both were shot.

The terrible cost of communism

Racing by a lot of interesting history, we come to the latter part of the 19th century and a pedantic slob known as Karl Marx. Marx never did an honest day's work in his life; he lived off the efforts of others, including his wife.

He plagiarized most of his boring economic philosophy from Hegel and, if he can be credited with any original thought at all, it was that all societies evolve into communist states after going through a phase of capitalism. But he later changed his mind about this, leaving him with NO original work or thought.

Armed with Karl Marx (and a few guns), Lenin came to power. It was not the Great October Socialist Revolution that you read about in American history books, but a simple coup d'état. The *real* revolution was the political one that occurred in February 1917, with the abdication of the Czar.

Eight months later, Lenin and his lieutenants seized power from the Duma in a near-bloodless coup, using more bluff and intimidation than bullets. They then murdered all their enemies and many millions who were not enemies, but were unlucky enough to have been born into the wrong class.

Contrary to our history books, the communists didn't "open up education to the masses." In 1908, a comprehensive, compulsory education system was inaugurated by the Czar. Around 10,000 schools were being opened annually. And listen to these numbers: By 1914, there were 7,500,000 primary schools, 819,000 secondary schools, and 80,000 universities in czarist Russia! The Bolsheviks continued the educational system built under the czars — but quickly converted it into an instrument of state propaganda.

One of the greatest perversions of history is that the communist revolution overthrew czarism. As we've seen, that isn't true. But what *is* indisputable is the terrible toll the Soviets then exacted. Their murder rate was so appalling, it makes the anti-Christian, anti-Semitic Hitler look like a parish priest. Here are the estimates Robert Conquest provides in his superb study, *Czarism and Revolution*:

Civil war following the Lenin coup	4,400,000 slain
Scientists and other professionals	160,000 slain
Bureaucrats and military	740,000 slain
Policemen	50,000 slain
Priests and other religious	40,000 slain
Peasants and workmen	1,300,000 slain
Cheka and other secret murders	2,050,000 slain
Government-induced famine	7,000,000 slain
Executed during collectivization	750,000 slain
Additional executions (NKVD)	1,600,000 slain
Intensification of Terror (1937)	1,005,000 slain
NKVD executions (1938-1947)	2,748,000 slain
Concentration camp victims	21,000,000 slain
Total killed	48,943,000 slain

And that doesn't include the millions killed in wars fought against China, Finland, Poland, Spain, the Axis in World War II, and others. Tens of millions of innocent peasants were slaughtered by the Communists. Entire villages, even entire races and countries, were eliminated. A total of 100,000,000 killed would not be an exaggeration.

Stalin, who took over after Lenin had a stroke, intensified the terror. He once bragged that he could break every bone in a man's body without killing him. He ordered the building of a canal from Lake Lodoga to the Gulf of Finland, connecting with the Neva River through St. Petersburg. One hundred thousand died on that one project.

That is some of the history I acquired during the long Russian nights. Quite different from what you've read before, isn't it?

Okay, I'll admit it: Except for Catherine's alleged sexual misadventure, I lied to you about the awesome sex you would find in this chapter. But it was for your own good.

Chapter Six

Governments Come and Go;
Bureaucracy Is Forever

It's October 12, 1992, and the temperature is six degrees below freezing (26 degrees F.). There is no heat in the apartments or offices of St. Petersburg. Heat is not authorized until November first. "You have a problem with that?" an official bellows. "Then wear your overcoat to bed!"

At the DHL foreign mail courier service, the girls are working at their computers with gloves on. To be fair, the early freeze caught everyone by surprise, as the wind changed and brought eastern Arctic blasts into St. Petersburg from Siberia. But socialist systems are inflexible, as well as uncaring, so there is nothing to be done about it.

You could burn your furniture to heat your flat. If you are out of matches, don't forget to take the empty match box with you to the match factory in Kirovskaya Oblast, because the factory is short of the boxes and, in 70 years of communism, they haven't been able to solve this supply problem. The beer vendors have the same trouble. You must bring them replacement bottles or they may not sell you any beer. Sometimes they will, sometimes they won't. It depends. On what? Who knows?

During the winter of 1992, the city experienced a severe sugar shortage. It happened while St. Petersburg was surrounded by literally *mountains* of sugar on freighters in the harbor. The freighter *Altair* docked on September 8. It began unloading *38 days later.* Two other freighters brimming with sugar stood at dockside for a month before unloading started; then it took 45 days to unload the ships. Tens of thousands of tons of sugar sat in ships, while within sight of these "sugar mountains," in St. Petersburg there was no sugar.

An occurrence on one of my train trips is another illustration of the rigidity and stupidity of the system. Two young men across the aisle from me were asked by the conductor for their tickets. They had no tickets, they explained, because there was a long line at the ticket counter. The train was leaving before they could get to the ticket window, but they were willing to pay, including a penalty.

"Nyet," the conductor said with considerable vigor, "you're getting off at the next station."

"But the next train isn't for six hours and it is urgent that we get home — why can't we pay you?" they implored.

"It is forbidden! Take your bags and come with me."

The boys clenched their fists as if to attack the conductor (a deadly error that would have put them in Siberia or wherever they put refuseniks in the old days — maybe North Dakota). Everyone in the coach began yelling at the conductor, letting off some of their frustration because of their own similar experiences. "Let them go" ... "Don't be an ass" ... "Stupid bolshevik" ... "Fascist" ... all of this from well-concealed mouths in a sea of vodka fumes, shabby coats, moldy back-packs, and muddy boots.

The proper totalitarian response would be to arrest the entire coachfull of enraged and exasperated people for "disrespect to an official of the glorious October Railroad." But fearing an attack by 100 snarling natives, the conductor called for help on his radio. Three more burleys appeared almost instantly; it was the only time I have seen the bureaucracy move with alacrity. The mob became quiet and the hapless boys exited the train at the next station.

Some of the ideological and commercial transformations seen in Russia today are startling and even amusing. At the Museum of Revolution, those hallowed halls where Lenin and his co-conspirators plotted and directed the coup against the czarist regime, advertising space is now being rented to a company that sells roulette wheels, crap tables, and other gambling paraphernalia.

Below a gigantic mural of the Bolshevik attack on the Winter Palace are samples of these gaming devices, including slot machines and a pretty blonde in a miniskirt who will explain how they work — and how rich you are going to get. Amazing!

You can still see Lenin's desk at the museum, along with cut glass containing revolutionary slogans and other artifacts of the Great October Socialist Uprising. But when you look up, you see a picture of a giant roulette wheel overhead. The beat toward capitalism goes on, even at the Museum of Revolution.

Yes, sometimes it seems like a Three Stooges comedy here.

Tokens take their toll

Try to make a call from a pay phone in Russia. It's a classic example of the planned economy. The only coin the pay phones will accept is the 15-kopek piece. Because of inflation, 15 kopeks is nothing, even to a starving Russian. It takes 25 of them to equal one penny. So phone calls are virtually free — *if* you have a 15-kopek coin.

But, as this is a socialist system, there are a few little problems. First, they don't make 15-kopek coins anymore. Why should they, when they are virtually worthless? Second, Russian pay phones don't work very well; they eat 15-kopek pieces voraciously. You need at least two, and sometimes three, to make a single call.

Because of this typical bureaucratic screw-up between *need* and *deed*, the 15-kopek coin has become a hot item; speculators sell them for 20 times their face value.

A similar problem exits with the subway system, and Yury Rezanov, a doctor, is using the discrepancy between supply and demand to (he hopes) get rich.

The great planners in that unseen office on the fourth floor of some building in which, I guarantee you, the elevator doesn't work, decided to switch to green plastic tokens instead of kopeks for the subway system. But the plastic tokens are so flimsy and so poorly made that they become deformed after one or two uses. (In fact, many come deformed straight from the factory.)

When you feed one of these deformed tiddly-winks into the toll monster, the toll monster becomes very angry. He spits out your offering and crashes giant metallic gates across your thighs. You're lucky to get out without a fractured femur.

Dr. Rezanov decided there was a market opportunity here. He bought a stock of these "plastic invitations to the orthopedic ward" and offered them for sale across from the subway entrance, marked up to five rubles each. Sales are slow now, but he thinks things are bound to pick up: "Now nobody wants to buy them because you can still buy them at the Metro station. But in the future they won't exist and children will want to look at them."

Why is a doctor peddling defective subway tokens on a street corner? Because he is desperately trying to make enough money to feed his family. He doesn't have the cunning (or the amorality) of the boys in the powerful Russian mafia, so he does the best he can.

Pity the poor farmers

As bad as life is in the cities, conditions are worse on the collective farms. The peasants, half-starved at times, live in a sea of mud for most of the year. There is no medical care; meat and dairy products are unavailable. To obtain sausage, butter, and eggs, the peasants have to make a long journey on a filthy train to a city in their region, purchase the food (which might be grown on their own collective farm) at state stores, and then haul it back to the village, often in sub-zero weather.

On the train from Moscow to St. Petersburg, I noted there were very few farm animals in the pastures we passed; a few goats, an occasional cow, but nothing else in the way of meat or dairy animals. The reason for this, I was told, is because the Soviet government forbade the production of hay in this area.

"Why," the farmers asked, "can't we grow hay?"

"You cannot grow hay because it is prohibited, that is why," came the reply.

The peasants wanted desperately to keep their farm animals, which were their main insurance against starvation. It was inconceivable that one could exist without cows, chickens, and pigs.

Now, while there was no hay, there *was* plenty of bread. In typical socialist fashion, bread was priced by the government far below its cost of production. It seemed logical to the commissars to sell bread for one cent a loaf; so what if it cost 25 cents to produce it at the collective bakery? After all, everyone needed bread. And the laws of supply and demand had been abolished by Lenin.

With bread being practically free, the farmers didn't need a degree from the Wharton School of Finance to know what to do next; they fed their cows bread from the collective bakery. The cows did just fine — until a severe bread shortage developed. This led to the inevitable: strict rationing of bread, and an even greater shortage of the staff of life for both man and beast. The law of the loaf, administered from the end of a Kalashnikoff automatic weapon, brought the crisis to an end — and with it, any hope the farmer had of keeping his livestock.

If a farmer attempted to grow hay anyway, he would be put in prison and his animals seized. So the horses and cows were killed and eaten. Now the peasants must spend a great deal of their time, and most of their money, trudging into the unfriendly cities to buy their sausage and butter (which is made in another region of the country, where hay production *is* permitted). Under communism, this all made perfect sense.

The sausage train

If you enjoy sausage, you would think it is better to live in an area where they produce sausage. If that makes sense to you, it proves you're not a Russian. If your area produces sausage, it stands to reason that *all* of it must be sent to Moscow or another distribution center so it can be made available fairly to all citizens. Of course you may buy some of the sausage — IF you can afford to buy a ticket to the city market and IF a ticket happens to be available.

The suburban trains to Moscow are a dark green color, which has led to a favorite joke among the people in the countryside: "What is long and green and smells like sausage?"

The answer, of course, is the train from Moscow.

Russians will line up to buy sausage from the long green thing, but that doesn't mean they *like* it. According to my friend Boris, Russians long ago gave up on a concern for the quality of food; as a result of centuries of starvation and semi-starvation, only quantity counts.

Oh, and about that sausage: If you toss a piece of it to a dog or cat, they will sniff at it, look at you as though you were trying to poison them, and walk disdainfully away.

Russian sausage is only about five percent meat; what the rest is no one knows except God, the workers at the people's "meat" cooperative, and those picky cats. Starving Russian scientists eat it, not because they are dumber than the cats and dogs, but because they have fewer options. Cats, being more independent than people, have a nice selection of garbage readily available in any alley. Nature tells them what to select; man is not so well equipped.

A mountain of fertilizer

One of the most preposterous examples of how the Russian farmer is not permitted to farm was the experience of a group of Finns who brought some of the most modern farm machinery to Russia. They assumed the only reason Russian farmers were producing potatoes the size of walnuts was because they didn't have the proper equipment.

When they arrived at the commune the government had "permitted" them to help, they were astounded to see something that indicated a far deeper problem than a simple lack of machinery: Behind the buildings was a mountain of cow manure three hundred feet high. It had roads going up the sides so even more of this natural fertilizer could be deposited at the top.

For miles around, the fields were starved for fertilizer. But the commissar in charge had ruled that it was "not permitted" to use the manure, furnished by their own cows, to enrich the soil to grow potatoes. The regulations were quite explicit about how the cow dung would be collected and stacked. There was no regulation about *using* it for anything, so of course no one could remove any of it. Rules are rules, don't you know.

The Finns threw up their hands in disgust, left the machinery, and went home. When the equipment inevitably broke down due to abuse and neglect, it was left in the fields to rust. As far as I know, it still sits there today.

Where are all the bananas?

If the communists couldn't organize the farmers to grow food, then you would think they could at least figure out a way to import food. But no; for years during the great struggle for the socialist paradise, bananas disappeared from the country. Now, Russians *love* bananas, and with the advent of the mafia version of free enterprise, bananas have returned.

Coolers, those large rooms for maintaining foods at a moderate temperature, are simply unknown in Russia. Bananas should be kept cool, not cold as in a refrigerator, but cool. Well, the Russians are nothing if not resourceful. After all, they've coped with a warped economy for the last 70 years.

For a small fee, bananas are warehoused at the various morgues around the city. This may seem a little macabre to you, but why not? Why waste all that refrigeration energy on a bunch of stiffs?

Communist "farm policy" probably reached its nadir under the rule of the ignorant and brutal peasant, Nikita Khrushchev. (An interesting footnote: He was so despised by his fellow Russians that for 20 years no one would dream of naming their child "Nikita.")

Khrushchev decreed that farmers should grow corn in the northernmost parts of the Soviet Union. A great deal of the Soviet Union is above the Arctic Circle and, Nikita reasoned, why should that land go to waste?

The farmers shrugged their collective (if you'll pardon the expression) shoulders and planted corn. They managed to grow plants that reached a height of 18 inches, but not one kernel of corn was ever produced. The farmers were undoubtedly punished for their lack of Stackhanovich zeal.

One of the most amusing stories I heard about the snaggle-toothed Khrushchev concerns a trip he took to Murmansk, about 200 miles inside the Arctic Circle up near the Norwegian border. You would think that even a native from tropical Samoa would know that you can't exist in a polar climate without heavy socks; your toes will freeze and fall off. But there were no socks in Murmansk.

Khrushchev was to give a speech to a large "volunteer" audience of Murmanskies, but before he could start his speech, there began a low chant that soon developed into a roar from the assembled thousands: "Noskie! Noskie! Noskie!" ("Socks! Socks! Socks!")

Thinking it was some kind of honorific, Khrushchev smiled his gap-tooth smile and waved at his admiring subjects. After someone finally summoned the nerve to tell Nikita what exactly the crowd was yelling, the grin vanished, and then so did Khrushchev. What happened to the Murmanskies, or to their request for socks, I never heard.

More good news/bad news

I mentioned that Soviet farm policy reached its nadir under Khrushchev. Something occurred in the early spring of 1993 that belies that assertion. The farmers on the collective found themselves without enough feed to maintain their milk cows. So the bad news was that 200,000 cows were slaughtered.

The good news was that the price of fresh meat plummeted, albeit temporarily. But the additional bad news is that there will be no fresh milk in Russia for the next 20 years, if ever. Milk will have to come in a never-ending river from the West to avoid extreme deprivation, especially among Russia's children. I'm afraid this isn't likely to happen, with refugees of war on three continents already crying for food.

Of course, if we try to send foodstuffs to them, we'll probably send the wrong things. A recent study published in the British medical journal, *Lancet*, reported that cat and dog food in advanced nations is more nutritious than the so-called food we give away. The typical ration sent to needy countries contains no meat, unlike the meat-filled chow of the lucky dogs and cats in America. The refugees and other unfortunates get a vegetarian mix of flour, kidney beans, vegetable oil, sugar, and tea. Your dog would look like a refugee, too, if he ate THAT every day.

Your typical Russian would love to have that dog food. They'd probably eat a nice plump dog, too, as long as it wasn't their own. Maybe our animal rights fanatics should get on this one: Start worrying about the millions of people starving to death and give Fido a rest.

Say you are a Russian and you are fed up with the socialist idiocy that surrounds you. You live in Provideniya, which is only a 50-minute trip to Alaska. Why not get a visa for a concocted "business trip" (a bribe should do it) and then defect?

There is a slight socialist problem. You will have to fly 11 hours to Moscow, at enormous expense and not inconsiderable danger (the only airline is the highly dangerous "Aeroflop;" more on it in a bit), to get a permit for that 50-minute flight to America.

Assuming you can afford it, and you get one, you must then fly another 11 hours back to Provideniya to get the plane to the promised land. You will have flown nearly half way around the world for a 50-minute hop.

But if you can afford it, there's no doubt it's worth it. Just ask any Russian.

Chapter Seven

St. Petersburg
and Her Ugly Sister

It's November 7 and St. Petersburg is covered with a fresh mantle of snow. This is the way the white lady should always dress — in a coat of ermine. The fresh snow acts as a magical face lift. The blemishes are gone; the stink of garbage, the flies, the mosquitoes are all forgotten. You forgive her faults, feel a little guilty for the criticisms of summer — and fall in love with her all over again.

The best time to walk this lovely city is around seven in the morning. The working people are not yet on the streets; the bureaucrats are sleeping late; and the thieves are cozy in their homes, counting their loot. The Italianate architecture, the many parks, the calm canals, and the ornate Russian Orthodox churches (the 20 percent left standing that survived the rages of Bolshevik atheism), are all yours to enjoy.

When you walk along Nevsky Prospekt, the main commercial avenue of St. Petersburg, be sure to look at the remarkable variety of faces you will see. There are about 120 different ethnic groups in Russia. Some of them will look quite strange to you, even grotesque. Semiconscious, weaving drunks are always in evidence, as are people of obvious quality and breeding. (I don't care what the liberals say; I'm convinced you will find people of quality everywhere — and also people with little good in them.)

Living in a Russian city is, in one respect, like living in a Dick Tracy cartoon. Are you old enough to remember the signs on the commercial establishments in that comic strip? Everything was generic: it was Drug Store, not Murphy's Pharmacy. It was Restaurant, not Cafe l'Europe. Walk down Nevsky Prospekt and you will see storefront signs that read Meat (miaso), Photo (fota), Fish (reeba), and Restaurant (pectopah). When the people own everything, and therefore nothing, all of the stores are generic. Even the *people* are generic, at least in the economic sense.

Occasionally, when walking on Nevsky Prospekt, I'll see something that reminds me that I am truly in a distant land. This morning a street band was playing old-fashioned American music, and playing it very well. A young delivery boy was doing the Nazi goose step to their rendition of "The Battle Hymn of the Republic." I wanted to throw him into the nearby canal, but of course if I did, he would have absolutely no idea why his antics were so offensive to me. (A lot of Americans wouldn't, either.)

The city in a swamp

Peter the Great built St. Petersburg on a marsh fit only for mosquitoes and the birds that eat mosquitoes. He imported Italian architects to design the city and thus created one of the great architectural wonders of the world — it is known, appropriately, as the Venice of the East. But the "great Russian architects" who built it have names like Tresini, Rastrelli, and Rinaldi.

According to legend, when St. Petersburg was founded, a monk was critical of the Czar's modern ideas and prophesied: "St. Petersburg will one day be empty." The Czar rewarded him for his dire prediction by having him "beat with a knout."

It has taken massive efforts to keep the monk's prediction from coming true. It seems there are always grandiose plans to revitalize the city. There have been no less than 30 such plans since the Great October Socialist Revolution of 1917.

St. Petersburg's present mayor, Anatoly Sobchak, is no exception to this tradition. He has promised to turn the city into an international financial and trading center; to open special banks for teenagers, so their meager funds will earn interest; to stop the engineers from meddling with the Gulf of Finland (their damned dams have ruined the natural drainage of the city and turned it into a beautiful sewer); to fight corruption; and, of course, to give the old lady a face lift that will restore her exquisite beauty.

None of these ambitious plans has materialized, perhaps because Sobchak spends 300 days a year abroad — at taxpayers' expense, of course.

Every 100 years there is a devastating flood in St. Petersburg that washes away everything except the buildings themselves. Soviet engineers decided they could outsmart nature, so they blocked the outlet of the Neva River into the Baltic Sea, so they could control the water's flow. Bad idea.

St. Petersburg still has periodic floods — it's nature's way of cleansing the marsh of nature's and man's detritus. Thanks to the meddling of the engineers, it also has canals that are now polluted, water that has to be boiled before drinking, and there are no fish left in the Neva, except for the annual desperate run for the sea by the korishna from Lake Ladoga. The people remain, but the fish have gone to more pleasant, capitalist waters.

In 1982, when the plans for damning up the Gulf of Finland were first discussed, Vladimir Znamensky, a Russian hydrologist, said it was a stupid thing to do. It would be like putting a plug in a bottle, he argued. It would destroy the city's natural drainage, leading to ecological disaster.

His warnings were suppressed by the Communist Party and the KGB, and he was fired from his job at the state hydrology institute. Now, industrial waste and raw sewage threaten the very life of the city. The brown water in the city's canals is loaded with industrial chemicals and intestinal parasites like *giardia lamblia*, the national animal of Russia (everybody carries at least a few million in their intestinal tract).

The city of St. Petersburg adds to the problem because its water sanitation methods are medieval. *Less than two-thirds of the sewage is treated at all before being dumped into the Neva River, which supplies drinking water to the 5 million citizens of the city.* Znamensky, in spite of persecution, still fights the dam construction. But even though the government now admits the dam has created an "ecological disaster," work on it continues. The only thing the Russian bureaucracy knows to do with a mistake is to compound it. Shortly before I left St. Petersburg, Znamensky was quoted as saying, "Either we destroy the dam or the dam destroys us." Of course there's a third possibility that's the most likely of all: The bureaucracy will destroy Znamensky.

The Big Potato

Moscow is as unattractive as St. Petersburg is lovely. The Big Potato, as it is called, is St. Pete's older ugly sister. For miles in any direction you see nothing but endless rows of tall, decaying concrete "dormitories" that house the proletariat, meaning everybody but the communist aristocracy.

The Muscovites have a phrase to describe their city: "Moskva — bolshaya derevnya" (Moscow — Big Village), which conjures up images of an uncivilized and grimy settlement in the middle of nowhere. According to one survey I saw, St. Petersburg was ranked as the eighth most beautiful city in the world. Moscow was listed as the 300th. (They must have only investigated 300 cities.)

When you compare the heaps of desolate concrete in "modern" Russia with the beauty of its czarist past, you can understand why many Russians would like to have the monarchy back. Life under the last of the czars, including Czar Nicholas II, was the best they had ever or probably *will* ever know. The government under the late czars was remarkably similar to our original American system before it was "democratized" by Woodrow Wilson. Only property owners and taxpayers were represented in the Duma (elected house); representation was through a system of electoral colleges. The system wasn't perfect, of course, but it was better than anything Russia has had before or since.

With the communist coup — the people never chose communism; it was imposed on them — came the ugly and depressing architecture of Stalin and Khrushchev, large grey or pale-yellow boxes, with a gaping square hole in the facade. All of the buildings look like post offices — or prisons.

After Stalin's massive and artless buildings came Khrushchev's "dormitories" — five-story buildings to house the proletariat. Khrushchev, an ignorant and vicious peasant, knew very little about architecture. He conceived the idea of combining the bathroom and the kitchen to conserve space, so the toilet was placed in the middle of the kitchen floor. Brilliant — only one sink was needed for washing the vegetables and for washing your hands.

That's somber Russian hyperbole, but I believed it after seeing the living conditions of the average Russian scientist. The room for the toilet is often so narrow that a very large person would have to back into it to sit down. Fortunately, you don't see many enormously fat people here — they don't get enough to eat. The somewhat fat older women, the babushkas, live on bread and potatoes and so look better nourished than they really are.

The concrete "dormitories," especially those built by that murdering maniac, Khrushchev, are like our prisons, except they're not as clean. The hallways are dark, dank, littered with trash and garbage, and smell of urine. Educated, cultivated Russians live in slums as filthy as any you will encounter in Caracas, Rio, or New York. Let me repeat, these are *upper class* Russians who must live alongside the lowest elements in their society. Remember, everyone must suffer equally.

Once you pass into the apartment of self-respecting Russians, it's a different world. Although cramped, it will be immaculate and quite pleasant.

Why don't the neighbors get together and clean the halls, do a little painting, and repair the sagging doors, you ask. If they did, they would run the risk of having their apartment snatched away by some parasite in the nomenklatur, who would give it to his newly wedded daughter or his mistress.

A moment of magic

Nikolai and I took the overnight train to Moscow, to visit Dr. Karandashov and learn more about his work with photobiology. We stayed in the apartment of a friend; it was the usual Russian habitat, vintage 1930, frozen in time for six decades.

When we went to the hospital the next morning, for a moment I thought I *had* been magically transported back to the 1930s. We entered the office of a professor Anatoly something-or-other, a tall distinguished-looking man, and it was like entering a black-and-white movie. There on the desk was an ancient monocular microscope, the kind you saw Louie Pasteur peering into, as if he were actually seeing something. Next to it was one of those old typewriters, with all the little metal arms that always got tangled if you typed too fast.

But most magical of all, there in the corner sat Greer Garson, looking demure, but somehow radiantly beautiful at the same time. Even her silver hair was cut in the flapper style. When she looked up at me, sparks of passion radiated from her eyes.

Greer — her real name was Natasha — came over and offered her hand. I wanted to kiss it and caress it, but I restrained myself. I felt myself falling into her large grey eyes.

I knew something special was happening. I felt like Humphrey Bogart. We would be trapped in a revolution. We would fight heroically and make love under fire. She would be injured in an explosion and lose the baby. I would smuggle her out of Russia to freedom in a gypsy's cart under a load of hay. I would escape detection by pretending to be a drunk deaf mute (something Lenin often did). We would crawl to freedom under a fusillade of bullets and make it to the Austrian border. We would lose consciousness in each others arms, to awaken in a sparkling clean hospital. There would be contracts for movie rights and we would live happily ever after.

After coming out of my trance, I asked Greer, uh, Natasha, if she would like to accompany Nikolai and me to the opening concert of the 1993 season of the Moscow Symphony that night. She accepted enthusiastically. Clearly, it was destiny!

After the concert, I knew I had to act fast, as Nikolai and I had to leave for St. Petersburg the following morning.

"Natasha," I asked, "would you visit me in St. Petersburg? I have a guest room or you could stay at the Hotel Europe. Swan Lake is at the Beloselsky-Belozersky Palace — we will have a wonderful time." (And, I thought, maybe the revolution won't start until you get there, and we could still be propelled into history.)

She reacted with surprise. "Oh, no, Beel, I couldn't possibly go anywhere without Anatoly. You must understand that."

"Anatoly? Who's Anatoly?" I asked.

"Why, Professor Anatoly Noske — you met him at the office today."

So I had.

Nikolai and I left Moscow on the early-morning train. It was a dismal day, with rain and fog to match my mood. I never knew it could rain and fog at the same time. Ah, well, another new Russian experience.

Hitler tries and fails

Back to St. Petersburg. Somehow this incredible city continues to defy the monk's prophecy. Even Hitler's mighty army and 40-degree-below-zero weather couldn't destroy it. The citizens of Leningrad were cut off from the world, starved and bombarded for 900 days. At the beginning of the blockade, the population of the city was 2.5 million. When the Soviet army broke through two-and-a-half years later, there were only 700,000 people left alive. Some had escaped, but a million and a half died of war wounds, starvation, and freezing.

During the siege, if someone went out to chop ice for water and fell on the slippery pavement, it was often a death sentence, as starvation had sapped the strength of people to the point where they could not get up. Death from freezing came in minutes.

The starving people ate anything and everything, including grass, roots, glue from the back of wallpaper, and book bindings. People boiled down their belts, oil, paint, medicine, spices, vaseline, and glycerine. They ate all the cats and dogs and even boiled their furs.

Criminal elements butchered corpses and sold the human meat for food. It was said you could always tell who the cannibals were, as they had glistening eyes, compared to the deathly white glaze of the protein-deficient population. Hitler said: "We don't need to storm the city. It will devour itself." But he was wrong.

Somehow, after nearly three solid years of daily bombardment, the city (or what was left of it) held. Hitler was unable to have his victory party at the Astoria Hotel as planned. (Ironically, today the Astoria is crowded with German tourists and businessmen from Frankfurt.)

Over 50 years after the greatest siege in the history of warfare, the survivors of the 900 days still receive special privileges (lifetime subway passes, discounted tickets to all state cultural events, extra money, going to the head of the queue), even if they were only foundlings at the time of the siege.

Images of America

I thought it would be obvious to Russians that I was an American, but that wasn't the case. They would guess everything from English to Swedish to German. One man said I looked like a German U-boat captain — I kind of liked that. (After all, I do look like Sean Connery, don't you think?)

All the propaganda they've heard notwithstanding, the Russians are absolutely fascinated with Americans. They think we are the cleverest, the most beautiful, the kindest, and the richest people in the world. Although they were told for 70 years that we were the scum of the earth, they think we are the cream of the crop.

But, I told them, things are now tough in America, too. For example, I said, many workers are being forced to economize by selling one of their cars. I'd get a dazed look:

"Did you say sell *ONE* of their cars?"

"Yes," I'd reply, "and it's very traumatic. But some families, if they have grown children at home, have three or four cars and it's not so bad for them."

There would be a shake of the head in disbelief. It would be comparable to someone telling you that every member of a Japanese family owned a Lear jet. If you think that is hyperbole, let me tell you that my dear friend and colleague, Nikolai Chaika, a 54-year-old educated scientist, is typical of millions of Russians professionals — he has never owned a car and, in fact, has never even driven one.

Another failure of the communist ideology that is worth mentioning: In creating a state of equal poverty for all, they did not succeed in abolishing the relative value system by which we all live. If you give a Russian a present, he will first say: "Oh, my, this was expensive. You shouldn't have spent so much money." And then he will ask, "How much did it cost?"

If you are friends, that seems perfectly natural to them. They are the most price-conscious people on earth — the exact opposite of the idealized Soviet man.

Reminders of the past

Vladimir Myayakofska was a highly esteemed writer and poet of the Great October Socialist Revolution. He wrote such gems as:

And even being the Negro
of elderly age
I would learn the Russian language
Without melancholy and laziness,
Just because Lenin spoke the language!

He was not only the Number One sycophant of the revolution, but a racist as well!

His profile adorns the wall of the Myayakofskaya subway station, down where the passengers get on and off. This mural is presented in bright red tile and is at least three times life size. There's also a base relief of him at the upper level, looking heroic and brilliant. These embarrassing reminders of the past are still there because there isn't any money to pay for removing them.

This display of defunct heroes is confusing to the young people of Russia. During the days of Myayakofska and Melinkov, everything was black or white: Lenin was good, the West was bad. In every institution throughout Russia, the first course taught was "The History of the Communist State." Now it is "The History of Mother Russia," but don't expect the message to be a lot different. The same teachers who were spouting communist propaganda in the '80s still lead the classrooms in the '90s.

What are they teaching now? No one is quite sure. The kids had a direction under communism. It was the *wrong* direction, but it was a direction. Now the guys know the only way to make a decent living is to peddle vodka and cigarettes on the black market. For girls, the quickest way to Easy Street is prostitution. Later I would see attractive Russian girls working as prostitutes in Istanbul; many of them had college degrees.

I'm afraid that having no clear ideology to replace the one they are now told was flawed is leaving a dangerous vacuum in Russia's young people — one that may, as in the case of Germany after their defeat in World War I, have disastrous consequences for Russia (and for the rest of the world).

Yesterday I saw and heard an unpleasant omen on Nevsky Prospekt that sent a numbing chill through me, far worse than the Arctic winds from Murmansk. It was a teenager carrying a "Puerto-Rican briefcase," one of those two-foot-long radios with two built-in speakers. He was blasting a sound wave of heavy-metal rock music that I was certain could be heard reverberating off the walls of the Peter and Paul Fortress, two kilometers away.

Another distressing and significant development was reported to me by a colleague in Moscow. He saw, for the first time, young adults shooting drugs in the subway. Can AIDS be far behind?

It must be time to move on. But where will I find another country sufficiently old-fashioned for my tastes — Bulgaria perhaps?

Meeting a young monarchist

While treating myself to a cup of real coffee at the Astoria Hotel, I met a young Russian named Alexander. As I mentioned before, the Astoria was where Hitler had planned to have his victory celebration. Built in 1905, the hotel has an ideal location — right across the street from St. Isaacs cathedral. In the old days, the hotel was the pride of the city. Now it's a three-star facility pretending to be four-star. But they make good coffee.

Alexander, about 27, has sharp patrician features and speaks excellent English. He had just returned from America and, it turns out, is a dedicated monarchist. I was surprised to find out there are a *lot* of young monarchists in Russia.

Imagine that — after 75 years of being told that the monarchy were enemies of the people who had ruthlessly exploited the workers, thus resulting in the Great October Socialist Revolution and the overthrow of their evil imperialist empire, many young people want the monarchy back. Obviously, some of the parents told their children the truth about life in the old days, even though they risked being shot for their counter-revolutionary behavior.

Or maybe the young people have simply decided that the present is so awful, the past must have been better. And who can blame them?

Chapter Eight

Drunk and Dangerous

No wonder Russian men drink so much. It's preferable to suicide. And for most of them, these are the only two ways they can escape the misery that has been heaped upon them. Communism has torn out the very heart and soul of most Russian men, especially those over 40. They see no hope of a better life and so spend their days in a drunken stupor. I have seen ambulance drivers at one of the surgical hospitals drunk at 10:00 am. By noon, a large percentage of Russian workers are so inebriated they are completely useless.

An astounding ten percent of the Russian population suffers from alcoholism, according to reports in their press. Three-and-a-half percent of all Russians suffer from delirium tremens (alcohol-induced central nervous system deterioration).

Ten percent of state revenues come from the sale of alcohol. That's more than is collected from their income tax. Because of high prices, samogon ("home brew") is made in such immense quantities that a sugar shortage has developed in the country.

Much of the samogon sold on the streets is dangerously contaminated with everything from anti-roach chemicals and methyl alcohol to gasoline. A litre of highly questionable Russian vodka costs about $1 on the grey market; export-quality stuff is $12 in the hard-currency stores. As $12 is more than a month's pay for most Russian workers, guess which brew they are going to buy.

Literary critic Vissarion Belinskii described his muzhik compatriots mercilessly: "Our people understand freedom as *volia!*, and *volia* means to make mischief. The liberated Russian nation would not head for the parliament, but it would run for the tavern to drink liquor, smash glasses, and hang the [landowners]."

I'll have more to say about the history of "little water" (that's what vodka means) in the next chapter. If I seem obsessed with the alcohol problem in Russia it's because it has a great bearing on the country's future. Alcohol seems to permeate everything; it's part of the national fabric. Alcohol consumption is the largest source of tax revenue for the present Russian government; it was the largest source of income for the communist government; it was the largest source of income for the czarist government. The country literally swims in alcohol.

In a land of the endless toast, it's not hard to understand why people are not unsympathetic to alcoholic coma as an avenue of escape from the harshness and injustice of Russian life. Is it any wonder that the life expectancy of the average Russian is the lowest in the West — and falling? Or that crime is skyrocketing?

Crime as a growth industry

The present instability in Russia has led to an even greater consumption of alcohol, which in turn has led to an increase in violent crime and accidents. Craig, a fellow American I met, was badly beaten by hooligans. He sustained a broken nose, a dislocated and fractured finger, and a knife slice across his abdomen. Fortunately, it was a slice and not a stab, so he didn't develop any serious leaks. He'll be okay. But I think it's time to tighten up my security.

I now carry my cattle prod (disguised as an umbrella) at all times — 120,000 volts has a very sobering and calming effect called unconsciousness. I also keep a German gas gun in my pocket that on inhalation causes immediate paralysis. Happily, I have not had to use either of them, yet.

I also try to avoid crowds larger than one person — the so-called Cacusians (pronounced "Kaw'-kaw-sons," not "Kaw-kay'-zee-uns") usually attack in groups. (If you saw them, you would immediately see that they are not what we call Caucasians — no one knows WHERE these brutish beasts came from.)

If I hear of one more case like Craig's, I'm going to hire a bodyguard. I think it might be worth the dollar a day it would cost me.

I also had installed, at a cost of $60, a solid steel door at the entrance to my apartment. It weighs 330 pounds and has a triple dead-bolt mechanism. It would take a professional safe-cracker or an anti-tank missile to bring it down. If I get iced, you'll know it was an inside job.

The major factor in the crime problem is the massive breakdown in law enforcement; criminals just don't get apprehended, much less punished, in Russia anymore. Sound familiar?

A Danish tour operator with years of experience in Russia is calling it quits. She says she just can't jeopardize peoples' lives for money. A quote by her in the *Moscow Times* is a succinct description of how the world in Russia has been turned upside down:

> How could it be that the police have become totally helpless? At the time of my earliest visits to this country, people were regularly imprisoned for writing poetry or speaking to foreigners. In those days the innocent feared everything. Now the guilty fear nothing!

How right she is. The criminal element is so much a part of the Russian system that it is difficult to see how it can be changed. It is far more pervasive than the drug cartels' control of Colombia — or Miami.

Russia's two mafias

There is a Red Mafia and a White Mafia in Russia. The Red Mafia is the communist party, elements of the army, and the nomenklatur (the most powerful, entrenched bureaucrats). The Red Mafia has had the economy in its grasp for most of the existence of the great workers' state. Its members have been robbing the people from within for 75 years.

The White Mafia is composed of the young men on the street who sell stolen goods at inflated prices to the struggling people. The state shops which sell at lower prices are often empty because goods have been diverted to the black market. This thievery could not take place without the tacit consent and cooperation of the Red Mafia within the government.

Here is how one former criminal investigator described the situation in the *Neva News* this year. It is as good a summary as you will find on the seemingly hopeless situation in this long-suffering country:

> The mafia has always been in power during the communist regime as well as today. Moreover, the "Red Mafia" intertwined with the "White Mafia" forms a dangerous conglomerate. The current influence of the criminal and political mafia is so high in this country that it is difficult to tell for sure who is governing Russia. In every office you will find a new nameplate, but the same person; he was a party member, but he is now a democrat.
>
> Believe me, nothing has changed anywhere. Maybe the situation has become even more scary. Before, our legal institutions were only communist party servants. Now the criminals who came to power are also the legal institutions' masters. These institutions, which are designed to protect us, are totally corrupt.

Is it any wonder the people have joined the mafia in a vicious tax revolt? In the middle ages in Europe, they used to lynch tax collectors. Russia is near that same salubrious condition today. In many parts of Russia, the revenuers are afraid to go out and collect taxes. Can you imagine that happening in the old czarist or communist police states?

The government is now sending out tax collectors with armed guards as protectors. They're needed to combat the *private* guards companies are hiring to throw the tax collectors into the street.

Some tax protestors have even broken into the offices of the tax collectors, to destroy files and dossiers. Now I am all for law and order, you understand, but hearing about a tax collector being beaten or his office trashed isn't the worse thing I could imagine. Anarchy is a bad thing, but sometimes it has its good side.

Many of the tax collectors are corruptible and will look the other way for a piece of the action. But in the unlikely event that you or the collector are caught, you face five years in prison, a penalty of double the unpaid taxes, and confiscation of your property: just like in freedom-loving America.

Late update: I just learned that, once he recovered from his wounds, Craig went back to New York City to live. He says it's safer! Now, that's what I call jumping from the frying pan into the fire.

I'll really miss Craig. He was arrogant and self-assured — my kind of guy. I sure wish he'd told me he was leaving. He had a gorgeous Russian girlfriend with long, coal-black hair. He could at least have left me her phone number.

Chapter Nine

Russians Will Drink *Anything*

At the Teblise, my favorite local eatery, it's hard to spend more than $2 for a good Georgian dinner. At the Petersburg Restaurant, which sticks up its nose at rubles, you can easily pay $50 for a meal. Twenty-five times the true market price seems a little excessive to me. The word has gotten out that Russia is not a bargain paradise, in spite of the desperate state of the economy. But you can get around the price-gouging if you live here.

At ten cents a bottle, beer is cheaper than water. And boy, does it pack a wallop! Some brands claim to be 12 percent alcohol — 24 proof. Everyone knows it's an exaggeration, the kind of hype you could go to jail for in the U.S., but it's cheap at any proof (and tastes like a very dilute solution of rusty nails).

I heard rumors that the much-beloved wheat vodka, a buck a bottle, was adulterated with rubbing alcohol. I asked my friend, Igor, about this. "No, Beel," he replied with some vehemence, "if you buy at the state stores, it will be absolutely pure. Only the street kiosks are dangerous."

I took a liter of the state-bottled stuff to Helsinki and had it analyzed. It was 25 percent isopropyl (so-called rubbing) alcohol. Serious vodka drinkers who can afford it are switching to medicinal (196 proof) alcohol imported from Europe. (You can see why it doesn't take long to get a party moving.)

Drinking the state booze may shrink your liver a little, but imbibing the petrol sold at the street kiosks can be fatal. One night in early February, the St. Petersburg police discovered a secret laboratory for vodka production in the basement of an apartment. The mini-distillery was remarkably well equipped, with labeling machines, bottling equipment, and, most importantly for a good bootleg operation, sophisticated corking and sealing machinery, so the bottles had properly sealed caps and *looked* authentic.

The police reported that the bottles were "filled to one half with some liquid from very dirty cans and then filled to the top with tap water." How many of the city's inhabitants, including the educated class, die yearly from poisoning of this sort is unknown. The price is right, so many people will continue to take the risk.

In January 1993, 4,000 bottles of acetone, labeled as Stolichnaya vodka, *and bearing all the proper state documentation of authenticity and quality*, hit the streets. The only reason a mass poisoning was averted was because the first bottles sold went to two Ruskies who, in the Russian tradition, opened the first bottle immediately upon leaving the store. They didn't want to wait a minute longer than absolutely necessary to get drunk on this fantastic bargain — a bottle of Russia's best vodka for only 40 cents.

One sip later and they knew this wasn't first-class vodka. In fact, it wasn't vodka at all. That's when the government quality control department was called in.

As acetone has a repulsive taste and corrosive action on the lining of the mouth, even a Russian wouldn't drink it straight. BUT HE WOULDN'T THROW IT AWAY. He would probably mix it with Pepsi, Fanta, or some similar all-American nutrient, and die with a smile on his face. The Sklifosovsky Emergency Medical Institute treats 30 to 50 cases of grave alcohol intoxication every day. These patients, many of whom die, are done in by the ingestion of acids, rubbing alcohol, pesticides, gasoline, kerosene, organic solvents, perfume, after-shave lotion, anti-freeze, and virtually anything else that comes out of a bottle and smells remotely alcoholic. They die from kidney failure, liver failure, respiratory arrest, or neurological complications.

But the cases reported from such facilities as the Sklifosovsky Institute are only the tip of the booze bottle. The government doesn't report the real story because many of the poisoners producing these lethal mixtures are leasing state distilleries at night. So the government is, in effect, in partnership with these merchants of death. According to the *Moscow News*, there hasn't been a single case of poisoning reported to the prosecutors office in Moscow. Not one. As the paper put it: "We are absolutely unguarded against the rascals who don't mind poisoning patrons. If we fail [to take action], we will never have a free market — there will be no buyers left."

In all spheres of business, the Russians continue to play Russian roulette with all the chambers loaded — especially when it comes to the sale of alcohol, an essential nutrient in the Russian diet.

Statisticians place Finland, Ireland, and France near the top of the list of countries with severe alcohol problems. I have been to these countries on numerous occasions and I am certain, from simply walking the St. Petersburg streets, that none of them has an alcohol addiction rate remotely as bad as Russia's. Sometimes careful observation beats statistics, in my opinion. But a downside on the Finns: They will challenge Russia for first place in alcoholism because they have such a terrible problem with alcoholic *children*. More on that later.

"We *inwented* wodka ..."

The Russians may have invented the light bulb, the airplane, and the telegraph, as they claim, but they didn't invent vodka. It was first imported into southern Russia in 1398 by traders from Genoa. Before the Genoans introduced "little water," which is what vodka means in Russian, the people didn't have much to do except work and die.

In the good old days before the introduction of vodka, Russians drank on only three occasions: the birth of a child, a funeral, and victory over an enemy. Even the weak alcoholic drinks that were available — mead, wine, and beer — were too expensive for all but the nobility to use on a regular basis. Vodka was just what they had been looking for.

By the 16th century, Russians had become serious drinkers and they haven't sobered up since, except for a brief period during the reign of Ivan the Terrible, who decided vodka was too good for peasants and forbade its sale. He only allowed his own retinue to get smashed.

Thus came into being the "kabak" — a true misfortune for the Russian people. By royal decree, Ivan had special houses built for drinking vodka and noble fooling around. As the government quickly realized, trading in vodka could be an almost inexhaustible source of revenue. So, it was decided, vodka-drinking wasn't too good for the common people after all. In no time at all, drunkenness became a national pastime. Even the princes of the realm opened up private kabaks to get a piece of the action.

One hundred years later, things were out of hand and the government attempted to restrict drinking. Naturally, this led to vodka revolts and the raiding of kabaks.

The party has been going on ever since. In the middle of the 19th century, there were half a million kabaks in Russia and, in spite of a lot of talk about the "national evil" of drinking, only twice through the centuries have serious attempts been made to curb the abuse of alcohol. The problem didn't seem to bother Catherine II, who said, "a drunken state is much easier to rule than a sober one."

Even worse than their vodka

As drinking is a hazardous pastime in Russia, a few more caveats are in order. The Russian beer is the worst in the world — even worse than Italian and American brews. One Russian described it, in a letter to the *Moscow Times*, as "donkey's urine." I can't vouch for that, but it is insipid, especially the bottles with the sediment at the bottom.

Avoid "wheat vodka," too. Although it is produced by the state, it can contain 25 percent rubbing alcohol. At least some of it did in the spring of 1993. Few people know what is really going on at the vodka factory. And a little Russian trivia for you: they don't make vodka out of potatoes and never did. I suppose they could as a last resort, but they don't.

So how do they make it? Let me put it in computer terms: garbage in — vodka out.

Also avoid the Russian "brandy." It is nothing but vodka colored with tea, coffee, or something worse.

Avoid all "Portwein," which is not remotely related to port wine and is strong enough to dissolve a metal subway token. If you drink the one labeled "eksperimentalny," you have a 40 percent chance of dying. On the positive side, you do have a 60 percent chance of living, but remember: That's less than your chances in Russian roulette with one bullet in the traditional six-shooter. There you have a 83.3 percent chance of the hammer *not* hitting a live round.

In any case, since all the printing on the bottle will be in the Cyrillic alphabet, you won't know what you're getting — and couldn't believe it if you did. So if you ever visit Russia, I suggest you confine your drinking to the hotel bar.

Worse than their vodka, part 2

Vodka is dangerous, no doubt. But the food in Russia may be even more so. Since 1992 and the opening of the street kiosks (which are run entirely by the Russian mafia), botulism, which is almost always fatal, has increased 700 percent. Salmonella food poisoning has increased 25 times. And for the first time in years, trichinosis has returned.

In the kiosks you can find bad meat, rotten fish, lethal mushrooms, moldy preserves, rancid bacon, beverages colored with any manner of chemicals, poisonous coffee, and chocolate that isn't chocolate.

Why do they ever do *any* business, you ask? Because at least they have *something* to sell — unlike the state stores, where you can stand in line for hours, only to be told that the last loaf of bread (or bottle of milk, or whatever) has just been sold.

Sausages, a staple in the Russian diet, are frequently stored side by side with footwear, cosmetics, detergents, pesticides, and insecticides. Shelf life of perishable foods is ignored. The Bodkin clinic in Moscow treated 833 cases of food poisoning in 1990, 940 cases in 1991, and 1,576 cases in 1992. Do you detect a trend here? And remember, probably less than five percent of cases are reported, as most people fear Russian hospitals more than they fear the food (and with good reason!).

That's why shopping in St. Petersburg is always such an adventure. How often can you shop for food and risk your life at the same time? It's just one of the wonders of living here.

It isn't any better in the countryside, either. Usually it's *worse*. Almost 100 percent of the people in the outlying areas have had typhoid fever from contaminated food and water. Most go untreated and either get well on home remedies or die. Most are listed as "diarrheal diseases," if they get diagnosed at all.

And if you think the food and drink sound dangerous, wait until I tell you about their hospitals! But first, let me tell you about my first real date in St. Petersburg — and how some damned fool almost killed her.

Chapter Ten

Bill "The Protector"

I was waiting at the bus stop one cold and windy Sunday morning and noticed a drunken Russian harassing a girl of about 18. One hardly notices the drunkenness because it is so commonplace, but I have seen very few Russian men, drunk or sober, pay any attention to the women.

The girl was clearly upset, by what I could only assume were lascivious remarks, and kept her attention on her book. This red-faced, bloated little man stared constantly at her profile, his stinking breath only inches away, and continued his slurred barrage.

When the bus stopped, before the dimwitted drunk could move, I stepped ahead of him and boarded the bus behind the girl. The bus was not crowded, so she chose a seat on the aisle. I motioned with my hands as I said, "Move over; I'll take care of him." I doubt she understood my English, but she understood the message and quickly slid over to the window seat.

The sot, in no way discouraged by my presence, leaned over me and started to speak to her. I motioned to him to leave and growled in English: "Go away and sit down — she doesn't want to talk to you."

He leered at me through his alcoholic fog. I glared back. I was unarmed and felt a little tense. Thankfully, his submissive peasant blood came to the surface; he lowered his eyes and sat down. But he continued to stare at me malevolently. The girl and I looked straight ahead.

When the bus stopped and he staggered to his feet, I grabbed the seat in front of me, ready to give him a well-placed kick should it become necessary. He turned and weaved his way off the bus.

The girl's eyes never left her book and she didn't say a word. At the next stop, I got off. There was no "spaceba" (thank you), no "pashalasta" (you're welcome). I passed her window and never saw her again.

There are few things in life that make a man feel more, well, manly, than helping a woman in distress. As I walked away, I felt ten feet tall. I don't know if my unknown Russian maiden appreciated what I'd done — but I did.

A few days later the weather cleared and the street bands were out again, playing in front of the subway station across from my apartment. Two old drunks were engaged in a heated argument, red nose to red nose, further fogging each others pickled brains with their high-octane breath. One had only one leg and was leaning on his crutch when the other drunk pushed him over. He fell to the pavement, his crutch clattering off into the street.

I was contemplating my Batman routine again when a nicely dressed, middle-aged woman stepped forward and commenced to berate the aggressor. He mumbled something and staggered off. She helped the one-legged drunk to his feet, retrieved his unbroken crutch, and sent him off in the other direction. My Batman cape stayed in my briefcase.

Later, I thought more about my reaction. Why had I even contemplated for a second interfering in an argument between two moronic drunks in a foreign country, surrounded by strangers who clearly perceived me as a rich foreigner, probably carrying what would be a year's pay for them in my pocket? For all I knew, the one-legged man deserved to be pushed to the pavement. I decided to burn my cape.

Greta and the lunatic Lada

The following week, I did meet one of those beautiful Russian women. But — surprise! — it turned out she wasn't Russian at all; she's an American from Alaska.

Greta is 21 years old and speaks English, Spanish, and Russian. I'm a little bit intimidated. At 21, I was still trying to master English.

In the 1840s, my family was pioneering its way from Virginia to Georgia, while Greta's family was making an even more adventurous move, to Alaska in search of gold. And here we are, 150 years later, meeting in St. Petersburg, Russia, both looking for adventure. It must be part of our common gene pool. Too bad I'm old enough to be her grandfather. But we'll be great pals, I'm sure.

For our first "date," I took her to every Russian girl's dream — a nice restaurant. We went to the Dom Architectura, the Architect's House, for dinner. It's located in one of the hundreds of mansions that line the streets of the old city; they're more like miniature palaces than houses.

Old Petrograd, as it was called, must have been a grand place to live — the evidence of its greatness is everywhere, reflected in the magnificent homes and palaces that line the streets in every direction.

I let Greta order; her Russian is much better than mine. The food was standard proletarian Russian: over-cooked meat of questionable ancestry, over-cooked vegetables, the usual "meat salad," which is mostly potato and mayonnaise, and undrinkable coffee. (We both agreed that missing good coffee was one of the biggest sacrifices in living here.)

The bill for both of us came to $6. I've been here long enough to realize it was over-priced. Ah, but the atmosphere.

The furnishings in Dom Architectura are late 18th century, with heavy red drapes and ornate gold trim at the borders of the ceiling. A huge crystal chandelier had somehow survived the invasion and the neglect of the common laborers who had lived there, compliments of the state, for 70 years. It felt like I was a guest in Dr. Zhivago's spacious home. Remember the one he returned to after the war, where he found his wife and family living in one room, the rest of the mansion being occupied by sullen and resentful peasants?

Uncannily, at that moment Greta said, "I suppose you saw the movie 'Dr. Zhivago' before I was born. I saw it before coming here and I was just thinking...."

It was amazing. I interrupted her and told her what she was going to say. We studied each other for an instant and then looked away. There had been, at that moment, a mental connection; it was like a mild electric shock, one of those "if only" things. But the mood quickly passed and it never happened again. I suppose that's a good thing.

On the way home, walking along the glistening wet streets, we narrowly missed becoming a headline in the morning paper: "*Two Americans Run Over Near St. Issac's Cathedral.*" As we were crossing the street near the statue of Nicholas the First, I caught a glimpse from the corner of my eye of a grey something coming right at us and moving very quickly. I stopped and yanked Greta backwards. A mud-covered Lada screeched past us, close enough to catch her handbag and send it flying into the night, the contents clattering in every direction.

Greta almost collapsed from shock. I held her closely for a moment. There was a barely perceptible tremble, but I knew she wouldn't cry; she's too strong for that.

"I think you saved my life," she said.

"We'd better get out of the street," I replied. "He may come back and try again."

Chapter Eleven

Heroes and Heartache —
The Russian Medical System

The medical situation in Russia is a sad dichotomy. The doctors at the top hospitals are competent and dedicated, despite being abysmally paid. But medicine for the common man, the exalted worker for whom the communist state was ostensibly created, is inferior to that found in many other Third-World countries.

Russia is, in fact, a *Fourth*-World country when it comes to delivery of medical services to the citizens of this "workers' paradise." This is not the fault of the doctors, but the failure of a system that places no value on human life.

A trivial but typical example of the conditions Russian doctors must labor under is the idiotic way that I.V. bottles are labeled. Bottles of I.V. fluid are manufactured with volume gradations marked into the glass. This is the system we used in the west 25 years ago, before the introduction of plastic bags. As long as you have to use bottles, it's a sensible way to keep track of the amount of fluid the patient has received.

But when the bottles arrive, you notice that the paper labels identifying the contents have been pasted directly over the gradations on the bottle. The doctor and nurse cannot see the volume indicated by the markings on the glass. So the nurse has to remove the label and reapply it on the back of the bottle.

Okay, you say, it's a stupid mistake. They'll get it right in the next shipment. No, they won't. Because the workers at the bottle factory have been doing it this way *for the past 50 years.* And no matter how many times you protest to the appropriate state committee, nothing changes.

Is it any wonder that when a Russian child is asked what he wants to be when he grows up, he replies, "a foreigner"?

Some remarkable heroics

The performance of Russian doctors during the great 900-day siege by the Nazis during World War II is a good example of the dedication and bravery of these underpaid professionals. The heroic, almost superhuman defense of Leningrad against the Nazis would not have succeeded if a major epidemic had broken out within the city. History is replete with examples of armies, and thus nations, going down to defeat due to the ravages of disease.

But during these terrible two-and-a-half years, with some of the worst winter weather in Russian history, not one major epidemic was allowed to add to the misery of the courageous inhabitants of the city of Peter the Great.

Think of it: 600,000 of the non-combatants starved to death. The dead and dying were everywhere. After a few months, medical supplies were not in short supply; they were non-existent. But there was no epidemic.

This remarkable medical and public health achievement was due primarily to the work of the staff of the Pasteur Institute of St. Petersburg, a department of the Soviet government not affiliated with the Pasteur Institute in France. The staff of 55 scientists and personnel resisted the temptation to eat their laboratory animals, although they were in a state of near-starvation. Instead, they continued their medical defense of the city against the ravages of pestilence which would, almost certainly, have been fatal to the resistance.

Every day these courageous defenders would go out into the city, which was under almost constant bombardment, to inspect and contain areas of infectious disease. Each day these brave souls knew it might be their last. But they persevered.

It was inspiring for me to stand on Pulkova Hill, 20 kilometers from St. Petersburg, and look across to the city, much as Hitler's generals did 50 years ago. Looking through their binoculars, they could see the streetcars pushing through the deep snow of the city, which was by then mostly rubble. They could see it, but they were never able to conquer it. The city's doctors, like everyone else, rode these streetcars, under fire, on a daily basis.

Ironically, out of this medical deprivation came one of the great medical advances of this century: The enhancement of the body's immune system through the irradiation of blood with wavelengths of light. There were parallel investigations in the United States and Germany in the 1930s, but the Russians made the greatest advances, out of the desperate need for a cheap substitute for antibiotics.

Russian scientists now have a massive accumulation of clinical data proving, beyond a doubt, the efficacy of this method of treatment. Over the past 20 years, they have treated thousands of cases of hepatitis, heart disease, and almost every type of infection, from pneumonia to peritonitis, with consistently good results.

When I came to Russia in early 1992, I thought I would be teaching my Russian colleagues about the clinical applications of ultraviolet therapy of whole blood. It did not take me long to realize that they were many years ahead of me. They were not only ahead in clinical experience, but their equipment was more sophisticated and even safer than my American-made instruments.

Using light, not drugs

I've already written an entire book about the incredible benefits of light therapy on blood (*Into the Light*, Second Opinion Publishing, 1993), so I won't try to repeat the whole story here. But let me summarize it for you.

Basically, while doing research on AIDS (which is a *collapse* of the immune system), I had come across references from the 1930s and '40s to a procedure that seemed to *stimulate* the immune system. It occurred when small amounts of blood were exposed to ultraviolet light. I coined the term "photoluminescence" to describe the process and had several instruments manufactured to provide the therapy. As you'll read in *Into the Light*, in case after case I experienced results so dramatic, they can only be described as "miraculous."

Tragically, research into this non-drug therapy was virtually abandoned in the United States when drug companies learned how to manufacture antibiotics in huge quantities (and for huge profits). This was not the case in the Soviet Union; there, the lack of antibiotics was a powerful inducement to continue to expand the uses, the techniques, and even the instruments of photoluminescence.

Most hospitals in Russia used the same basic methodology I did: A small amount of blood was removed from a vein, passed in front of the light apparatus, then returned to the body. I noticed one big improvement at once, however: The procedure I was using required that blood be withdrawn in a syringe, carried to the instrument, treated, then returned to the body. The Russians had advanced to a closed system; that is, blood was removed, treated, and returned to the body in one continuous procedure. The Russian method clearly was a vast improvement.

Soon after my arrival in St. Petersburg, Dr. Chaika, my wonderful seagull, told me that some of his colleagues were working on a method of irradiating blood that didn't even require removing any of it from the body. I said, "Show me!" So off we went to visit Hospital 15. It was a trip that showed me the worst of the Soviet bureaucracy — and the best of Russian medicine.

Amazing advances in light therapy

To get to Hospital 15, you have to go halfway to Siberia, or so it seems. First, we took the east-bound subway as far as it would go. Then, we changed to a rickety old bus, bulging with four times as many riders as seats. At the end of the bus line, we continued by foot for several hundred more yards, walking on slippery, frozen streets that frigid morning, until we came to the concrete maw that was the entrance to Hospital 15. (I've had to suffer a lot to write this book, from stench and mosquitoes to sub-zero Arctic winters and abuse from drunks. But you probably don't care.)

As we approached the entrance to the ten-story hospital, three reeling, terminally drunk men were leaving the building, heading for the vehicle depot behind us. It was 10:00 am and they were going to work — they were the ambulance drivers. (Policemen are sometimes seen in a similar condition.) We carefully negotiated our way around these protectors of the nation's health, emergency medicine's first line of defence, and entered Hospital 15.

As with many of Russia's scientific institutions, the elevators were "temporarily in a state of repair," which means permanently unworking, so we walked up seven flights of dirty, unlighted, and freezing-cold stairs to the clinic of Drs. Dutkevich and Marchenko.

In spite of their very limited resources, these two doctors are doing some very creative work here. Although it sounds like "Star Wars" medicine, their procedure is actually relatively simple. In their technique, an intravenous drip is applied in the usual way in a large vein in the arm. Then a fiberoptic thread is run down the tubing until it emerges just past the tip of the needle.

Once the fiberoptic thread is in place, it is a relatively simple matter to beam *light* down it. In fact, you can select which frequencies you wish to use; Drs. Dutkevich and Marchenko say they are having their greatest success with red laser light.

It is remarkable to see this application in use. The skin actually glows at the point where the needle has been inserted and for almost an inch beyond. I know some scientists say light can only penetrate the skin for a few millimeters. Once they have witnessed this procedure, they will realize they were wrong. I was absolutely fascinated by it, and stayed to watch three other treatments being given.

All four patients I observed seemed to be perfectly comfortable. There was no evidence of toxicity during the course of the therapy. Although Russian critics of this intravenous phototherapy claim most emphatically that it is highly dangerous and fraught with many side effects, Drs. Dutkavich and Marchenko told me they rarely see any side effects and absolutely none of a serious nature. (None of the critics I talked to during my year in Russia cited any examples of adverse reactions, but they were convinced of the dangers nonetheless.)

Clearly, this is a field of study that merits much further investigation. One of the huge advantages I can see to this form of photoluminescence is that, by directly injecting light energy into the blood, the entire blood supply can be irradiated in one treatment. Incidentally, as far as I have been able to determine, not one word about this procedure has been reported in the American medical literature. At best, this technology is five to ten years away.

Drs. Dutkavich and Marchenko discussed their use of intravenous light therapy at a scientific conference that was held in Saransk, about a thousand miles east of Moscow, in central Russia. Because of the historic nature of the conference, and the voluminous amount of light research reported from it, I asked one of my colleagues if he thought I should visit the city. He replied: "Not if you can possibly avoid it." For once I listened to good advice and avoided it.

Wonderful doctors in a dreadful system

The paradox between the cutting-edge scientific investigations being done by dedicated doctors and medical researchers in Russia, and the inability of the system to maintain even a modicum of modern infrastructure for their pauperized scientists, struck me again and again during my year in St. Petersburg.

For example, I visited the clinic of Dr. Aza Rockmonava, St. Petersburg's premier AIDS expert. After trudging up the usual multiple, dingy staircases (I don't think I ever visited a clinic that was located on the first floor), we were confronted with a massive door made of a bamboo-like material; it would have been right at home in many shacks I have visited in central Africa.

In fact, the conditions at most of the best Russian hospitals are only a little better than those I've encountered in central Africa. The conditions in the hinterland of Russia are *worse* than Africa. The reason for this is that the Africans have had the advantage of well-equipped Christian missionary hospitals for the past 50 years, something the communists would never permit in Russia.

In Russian village clinics, for example, urinary catheters are reused until they fall apart. They are not sterilized between patients; but it wouldn't matter if they were, because they are lubricated with olive oil.

But at least there has been *some* progress. Under the old system, many times medical people acted as though they didn't care. This wasn't true — Russians can be very caring and medical workers are no exception — but there was little they *could* do for most patients, as there was often no medicine and only old, broken equipment to use.

A physician in the Siberian town of Tyumen confirmed that things are better now than they were in the past. "In fact, today we are better off than ever," he acknowledged. "Back in the '70s we were short of everything, even penicillin."

When asked what they did, he replied: "We simply didn't administer it to those who needed it. Doctors were forbidden to prescribe it." Then he added, "If you ask about changes for the better, there have been some. Today one can go to Australia."

There is a laser research institute in the center of St. Petersburg that is an even more dramatic illustration of brilliant scientists working in buildings that are little better than cow sheds. The Institute of Precise Mechanics and Optics is located in a 19th century structure under which the planners of the Brave New World decided to build an extension of the St. Petersburg subway. The construction crew neglected to reinforce the building adequately before they dug under it, however.

As a result, the building started sinking into the hole they had created. After the building had buckled in the middle, with giant cracks running the length of it (it looks like it has survived a major earthquake), *then* the authorities decided to reinforce it. The structure would have been condemned and torn down in any western country; in typical Russian socialist fashion, it was business as usual in this building that almost cracked in half.

The scientists there are accustomed to catastrophe. They continue their research on the effects of laser light on biological systems as enthusiastically as ever. As you have probably guessed, the elevators there don't work, either. In fact, in all the engineering-type buildings (optical research, laser research, equipment assembly, etc.) I visited during my year in Russia, I only saw *one* with a functioning elevator.

Even the ones that worked scared the dickens out of me. One day a colleague and I were ascending in an elevator that did work, albeit with great groaning, lurching, and some strange clicking noises that sounded like electricity trying to break free. (Again, I didn't touch anything.) I asked my companion how often the elevators got inspected. He replied that he had never heard of one being inspected. Not EVER. Not a very comforting thought.

Can you imagine hospitals with non-functioning elevators? If the elevators don't work, how do you get a severely injured patient to the operating room on the tenth floor? (The answer is, with vast effort and discomfort, and no little danger to all parties involved.) In a land where there is talent aplenty, but little technical accomplishment, it makes you wonder what else is not working properly — the respirators? The defibrillators? It made me realize that there is a clear and present danger just *living* here, especially if you are over 60.

When outside elevators gained popularity back in the '60s in the U.S., the Soviet planners quickly decided to copy the idea. (I'm sure one of them claimed to have invented it.) Hundreds of these glass-enclosed leeches were attached to 100-year-old buildings that had no elevator, not even old broken ones, on the inside. These elongated metallic tumors look anachronistic and pathetic. And of course, almost none of them work.

The Church of Spilled Blood

Speaking of "temporarily in a state of repair," let me digress from medical stories for a moment (they're all pretty depressing) and tell you about the Church of Spilled Blood. This lovely and classical Russian orthodox structure was built in St. Petersburg in the early 20th century to honor the memory of Czar Alexander the Second, "the Liberator." He was murdered by an anarchist in a bomb explosion where the church stands now.

The Church of Spilled Blood has been "temporarily in a state of repair" for a very long time. When I was in St. Petersburg in 1965, it was covered with scaffolding. When I returned 27 years later, it was *still* in its wooden cage.

But in the fall of 1992, the authorities ordered the outside scaffolding removed. The restoration workers who had spent a great deal of their lives in returning the church monument to its original exquisite condition were astonished at the order, as their work was not completed.

Although all comrades are equal in a socialist state, some are more equal than others. You do as you are told or risk severe punishment — such as losing your job. The scaffolding came down.

A few weeks later, the workers were told it was all a big mistake by some faceless bureaucrat, which they had already surmised, and they were ordered to replace the scaffolding. I rushed to take a picture of the church, as it will probably be the last time this century it will be seen outside its wooden prison. (But then again, they might not get the scaffolding back up until the next millennium.)

An interesting sidelight to this restoration story: When inspecting the dome of the church, 100 feet above the marble floor, workers discovered one of Hitler's unexploded artillery shells nestled comfortably under a metal support. It was removed *very* carefully and without detonating, I'm happy to report.

Another elevator stops working

The Pasteur Institute occupies one of the newest buildings in St. Petersburg; it was completed in 1989. The elevator on the east end of the building gave up the ghost in May 1993, a four-year record of successful ups and downs. It didn't crash; no one was hurt, thank goodness. It just stopped working.

The elevator on the west end was still functioning when I left Russia, but was doing double duty. When that one goes, all medical supplies, foodstuffs, personnel, and honored dignitaries will make their way by that time-honored socialist invention, the stairway.

Russia's thousands of broken elevators seem to me to be a perfect symbol of that vast nation's socialist failures: they are going nowhere and are all "temporarily in a state of repair."

Elevator update: Saw Nikolai at a medical meeting in Helsinki a few months after leaving St. Petersburg. "How is the west-end elevator doing?" I asked. "It quit two weeks after you left, Beel," was the reply. And he added with a straight face, "It's in a temporary state of repair."

The director of the Pasteur Institute announced that the west elevator had been closed "for reasons of the economy." Sure. So now human pack animals — in the form of Ph.D.s, mostly female — will haul laboratory equipment, experimental animals, and supplies up five miserable flights of dimly lit stairs.

Trapped in a time warp

A personal experience, spanning almost 30 years, is illustrative of the deep freeze Russian medical science has been in due to the oppressive influence of communism. I was a visitor at the Bodkina Hospital and the North Surgical Hospital in 1965. I went with a delegation of orthopedists in order to determine for myself if the propaganda we were getting in the West about the superiority of Russian medicine was really true.

Both hospitals were in buildings that were constructed before World War I. And apparently no improvements had been made to either building since they were first completed. As soon as I walked in the door, I was struck by the lack of modern equipment of any kind. There was nothing but iron beds like those Florence Nightingale attended in the Crimean war. The lighting was dim and there was no evidence of oxygen, respirators, EKG machines, or anything else that we in the West take for granted. There was one bathroom for a ward of 20 patients. It contained nothing but a sink and a filthy toilet. Ugh.

But here's the amazing part: When I returned to the Bodkina Hospital in 1992 — 27 years later — NOTHING HAD CHANGED. It was as though I had left only the day before. There were the same creaking doors, the same iron beds, the same filthy toilets. Only the feces were new (maybe).

In 1965 we had joked about a turnstile, inside a little enclosure, that one had to pass through to enter the grounds of the Bodkina Hospital. It served absolutely no purpose. There was no guard attending it; it didn't record anything; it was just there.

And it's *STILL* there. Nikolai warned me that, although it was useless, it was not entirely benign. If you were not careful, it would catch your heel and rip your Achilles tendon. I was careful.

Imagine being a doctor trying to do your life-saving best in these circumstances. It boggles the mind, doesn't it? But every doctor I met in Russia simply takes it for granted.

Chapter Twelve

Your Soviet "Partner"

The weather is always terrible in Peter's drained swamp by the Gulf of Finland. It's too hot, too cold, too rainy, too humid — and usually too windy. Because of the weather, maintaining the city's architectural treasures would be difficult even in a prosperous capitalist society. Under the communist freeze, it was impossible. The evidence of decay is everywhere. There are so many gutted buildings that you would think World War II ended just yesterday.

Ironically the ghostlike structures seen on every street, lovely buildings without windows, were not the result of Hitler's bombardment. They were caused by an attack of the Soviet bureaucracy, which was applying one of its famous five-year plans to the refurbishment of the city. In order to justify a large budget, one must have a grandiose plan. So the planners proposed that *all* buildings in the city in need of repair should be gutted and then restored. The "five-year plan" was approved and the buildings were stripped of everything, including the windows.

That was 40 years ago, and nothing much has happened in the way of repairs since. That's why so much of St. Petersburg looks like Hitler just left. As one of the St. Petersburg newspapers put it, "The city looks as if it has just endured an enemy occupation." John Kenneth Galbraith and other college liberals should learn from this socialist fiasco. But they won't.

When you're the new kid in town, and don't speak enough Russian to ask a beautiful young woman her name, there's little to do other than work. When I didn't feel like working, I'd sit at a cafe reading the latest copy of the *St. Petersburg News*.

One of the best ways to get to know a city and its people is to read its press. I can't read Russian, but there are several English-language papers in St. Petersburg, and some of them made for great reading.

A lot of what I read was good old-fashioned tabloid trash. There's something universal about human nature; the tabloids here are as weird and wacky as any in the United States. Except for the Cyrillic language, you can hardly tell the difference between those in St. Petersburg, Russia and those in St. Petersburg, Florida.

What entertainment! One of these Russian rags calls itself "The Very Scary Newspaper." Another one is *Klukva*, which means "nonsense." Russian tabloids have reported talking spiders, a vampire cat, and killer cockroaches. One had a story about a Romanian who has invented a time machine that will transport one to the Stone Age. They claim there are lines waiting for the trip, as some Russians will do *anything* to get out of their "workers' paradise."

Another story, complete with photos, was about a cheating husband who was turned into a dog wearing pajamas. The way they adore dogs here, it was probably a good career move. *Evening Moscow*, a thriving daily, recently reported that a black cloud of negative energy had descended on the apartment of Ruslan Khasbulatov, one of the more obnoxious members of Parliament. It is said to be similar to the evil force suspended over Lenin's tomb. Now THAT I can believe.

The artists' "partner"

There is no doubt that things have improved since peristroika for the Russian artist. But the Soviet mentality still weighs heavily on them, just as it does on everybody else in the new Russia (which is, in many ways, just like the old Soviet Union).

In "the old days," before 1988, an artist would be severely punished for not following the party line with his art. As long as your painting contained a hammer or sheath of wheat and a well-fed Russian Stakhanovich worker with a noble expression on his Aryan face, you could paint to your heart's content. (Curious point about that noble worker's face: The Russian peasant has blunt features that are distinctly *not* Aryan; but in glorified, official Soviet art, they all look like German storm-troopers.)

Deviate from the norm and you got five years in prison and another five years exile to Siberia. That's what happened to poet Joseph Brodsky, who won a Nobel Prize in 1968. I dislike most modern art, but I thought the penalties were pretty severe. Five years exile to Detroit, it seems to me, would have been punishment enough.

Russia is replete with artists. The painters are world-class and one can buy Russian art of the finest quality quite reasonably, for $50 or less. But when you get to customs, you'll get a harsh lesson from the Russian bureaucracy: They will demand that you pay a 500 percent duty on your little treasure.

Think of it: The painter makes $50 for his work and the government takes $250. But, as many liberals in the U.S. would tell you, the government has to tax the people heavily, since the bureaucrats will spend the money much more intelligently than the people who earned it. Lenin said the same thing.

A happy postscript: I just learned that the export tax has been reduced to "only" 100 percent. Now the artists are "equal partners" with the bureaucracy. The artist does all the work, takes all the risk, and then splits the profit with his benevolent superiors. Sounds like the U.S., doesn't it? No wonder I get discouraged and a little depressed, when I see slavery glossed over as welfare and witness what may be the future of our own country. (What am I saying? That is the PRESENT in our country — the future may be WORSE.)

At the turn of the century, under the rule of the much-maligned czars, Ten Pushkin Street in Moscow was a cultural center of the "Silver Age" of Russian culture. With the advent of "The Great Socialist October Revolution" in 1917, Ten Pushkin

Street was given to the ennobled workers and crammed with peasants, street cleaners, drunks, and other deserving supporters of the Great Experiment. Personal artistic expression was dead. The building rapidly deteriorated into a slum similar to what you can see today on New York's lower east side.

In the spring of 1989, the Moscow Soviet decided to "renovate" the building and everyone was thrown out. (What the government giveth, the government can taketh away.) That usually means a death sentence for any building, because they are immediately stripped of everything, including windows, and are reduced to hollow boxes exposed to the elements.

Miraculously, some repairs were done and the building was returned to at least its former dilapidated condition. Because of the great artistic history behind Ten Pushkin, 120 artists quickly moved into the vacated structure.

In spite of the fact that the water, electricity, and heating are often off, the building is a swirling pot of pent-up artistic talent. In the past three years, over 10,000 paintings from this one shabby, but historic, building have been purchased. They have sponsored over 40 major art events, including a concert to mark the 50th anniversary of the birth of the god of late-20th century music, the notorious drug pusher, John Lennon.

The Free Culture Foundation managed to smuggle the works of 20 modern artists aboard the Soviet space station "Mir," so they can now rightfully claim to have sponsored the first art event in space. Although I think most modern art *belongs* in outer space, I admire their courage and ingenuity in the face of terror and deprivation.

More efforts to renovate

Another group of artists, writers in this case, decided to go the "free enterprise" route. They purchased what can only be described as a dump from the city. Technically, it probably does not even qualify as dump, because that word implies a squalid building that can at least be lived in. These writers, some of them world-famous, had bought a structure with nothing but the outer walls standing. They commenced to put in windows and floors and the other fixtures necessary to survive the often cruel Russian winters.

The local Soviet found out about the sale from the Moscow government to the writers and went into a collective rage: "Living quarters sold on the open market? Never! Living space must be *assigned!* What about the people who are waiting for us, the Soviet, to give them an apartment?"

The attorney for the writers tried to explain to the ignorant and power-mad peasants in their grey, tight-fitting polyester suits that the sale had nothing to do with their precious Soviet. The writers were not asking to be put in line for an apartment 20 years hence. They had paid big money for their precious hovel and intended to use it as they saw fit. If the Soviet thought they owned it, they could go to court and let it be decided there.

"What court?" they declared. "We are still the masters in this neighborhood!" The worried writers asked the attorney what they should do. He advised them to prepare for war: build an iron fence around the construction site; put burglar alarms around the perimeter; attach high-voltage electric current to the iron fence; and hire guards in combat fatigues, preferably with German shepherds.

Can you imagine having to do that to protect yourself from your local *government?* From punks, drug addicts, burglars, and welfare brats, sure. But not from your county commissioners.

The attorney also advised, "If one of the dogs takes a chunk out of some deputy's behind, I will personally be very glad — let them learn to respect other people's property."

Until these Leninist louts die out, are voted out, or are shot by an irate and long-suffering public, Russia doesn't stand a chance. They are typical of the old Russian joke about the mentality of Russian peasants: "Every American wants to make money and have a son to carry on the business. Every Frenchman wants three wives and four mistresses. Every Englishman wants to be a nobleman and have a son graduate from Oxford. Every Dane wants to die at a party. Every Swede wants to die properly dressed. All the Russian peasant wants is to see his neighbor's cow die."

That's why even strong leaders have a difficult time ruling Russia. Weak ones have about as much chance as a blind motorcyclist. It's not politically correct to say that some people don't seem adaptable to a system of self-government, but I think it's true. Argentina and the Philippines are good examples, although lately there have been some signs of hope in both of these countries, too. Some countries change, in spite of thousands of years of despotism (Japan is one example), but sadly, they are the exception.

Chapter Thirteen

Escape to Finland

Retail clerks in Russia can drive you to fantasize about murder. I was reading my *Moscow Times* a few days ago in the coffee shop of a St. Petersburg hotel when suddenly all the lights went out. No, a transformer hadn't blown; the counter girl had turned off the lights so that she could better see her favorite soap opera on television.

When I first arrived in Russia, I had the naive idea that shopping would work the same way here as it did in the States: you indicated what you wanted, paid money for it, and got it. Not in the workers' paradise!

When you buy a train ticket to Moscow, after standing in line for an hour, you are told you can't buy the return ticket. Their job is to sell the ticket TO Moscow. Whether you get back or not is of no concern to them. And don't expect any "super-saver" fares, either. If you want to buy a ticket in advance, you'll pay *extra* for the privilege.

All public transportation in Russia is deplorable and dangerous, but a bus ride in a Russian city is an especially unforgettable experience. The crush of people — my glasses got smashed in my shirt pocket on one ride — is standard for Third-World countries like Russia. But there is an added element to the Russian ride that I have not seen anywhere else: The busses have such poor suspension that on curves, they sway like a boat and feel as though they are about to turn over. I asked my friend

Vladimir about this, and he replied with a grin, "Sometimes they DO turn over, Beel!"

It didn't take me long to decide I didn't want to ride the bus. Besides, I had learned how to bargain with the outlaw taxis (EVERY car in St. Petersburg is a potential outlaw taxi; just flash dollars at the driver) and found I could go anywhere in town for a buck. That's a hundred times the cost of the subway (one penny a trip), but it was a lot easier on my health (subway riders always have colds; I caught one a month until I stopped riding with them) and my imagination (as we travelled under the Neva River, I always visualized the walls caving in. The headline would read: "North line to Gorkiskaya floods in collapse of tunnel under Neva — 500 dead includes American wearing cowboy hat").

One time I took a friend out for a bite to eat at noon and the restaurant was CLOSED FOR LUNCH. I had to get out of this surreal place once in a while. You can understand that. The nearest outpost of civilization is Finland, so I go there to recharge my batteries, fatten up my body, and clear my mind of the resentment and frustration I feel when dealing with the detritus of the Great October Socialist Revolution.

Flying Russia's unfriendly skies

On one of my escapes, I wanted to get to Finland in a hurry. I debated flying there — until I read the latest mortality figures for Aeroflot, "the world's biggest airline." The previous year, 23 planes in the Aeroflot fleet had fallen from the sky. Russians refer to it, not so affectionately, as "*Aeroflop.*"

Once the world's largest airline, the carrier has now been broken up into 15 little Aeroflots. They have strange names and are under the direction of "Ministers of Aviation" who probably know more about managing a herd of yaks than running an airline.

With Aeroflot's transition to a profit-making business, their reputation as the world's worst airline has taken on a new dimension. Spare parts are available for hard currency only and, as the airlines have no hard currency, they make do with what they have — or just leave the part off. One can do without window shades, arm rests, and even toilet seats, but valves and switches are another matter.

It was recently revealed that the old communist tradition of bribery is still alive in the aviation industry. Passengers (many of them smugglers) bribe baggage handlers to allow additional weight. For $10 or $20 U.S., pilots sign off on the bogus weight lists. But the amount of runway required to take off is based on the weight of the loaded aircraft. If the total weight is incorrectly computed and the plane is too heavy, and thus enough power is not available for lift-off, the plane will roar into the ground just beyond the tarmac at 150 miles per hour and everyone will die in a big fireball.

Ironically, the price of taking one of these Adventures in Flight is soaring. A ticket from Moscow to Khabarovsk increased from 4,000 rubles to 25,000 rubles, so only the elite will be able to enjoy these closed-casket specials. But in truth, no one who knows what is going on will fly Aeroflot if they can possibly avoid it.

If you are thinking of flying with Air Uzbekistan, do your kids a favor and take out extra insurance. Also, bring fireproof dental records along with your passport and visa. As they say in Russia, "schastlivogo polyeta" (Have a nice flight).

North of the Arctic Circle

On my last pig-out visit to Finland (I can't make it on Russian food. I don't know why; it seems to work for them), I decided to visit the Arctic Circle. It's easier than it sounds; you go north from Helsinki to Oolu on the Gulf of Bothnia, then take the fast train to Rovaniemi, which is just a few miles south of the Circle.

In most parts of the world, crossing the equator is a big deal. In Africa there's usually a monument announcing the spot on both sides of the road. If it's in a town, they'll paint a line across the street. If you're on a ship that crosses the equator, the captain will ring the bell, make an announcement, and someone will buy a round of drinks.

But in Finland, there was nothing, not even a stick in the ground, to mark the Arctic Circle. I made my way across it (I think) and went back to Rovaniemi to warm up.

It's hard to believe that you'll find a town as modern as Duluth or Dubuque sitting on the Arctic Circle, but Rovaniemi is one. The windows in the hotels are triple-paned, but otherwise you'd never imagine the temperature drops to 40 below zero (that's 72 degrees below freezing — not counting the wind-chill factor).

These people are not Laplanders; you have to go even further north to see them. The citizens of Rovaniemi are Finns with some interesting characteristics. For example, they seem determined to smoke and drink themselves to death. Fortunately, their diet is very high in animal fat, which I suspect protects them, at least partially, from their libatory and respiratory folly.

There's a difference between a Finnish drunk and a Russian drunk you might keep in mind. If a Russian drunk fixes his eyes on you and is a little too close for comfort, you say in a loud, gruff voice, "What the hell are you staring at?" He'll waggle his palms at you, give you a rotten-tooth, nicotine-stained smile, and shuffle off to Berezovo muttering "nea problema" (no problem).

A young drunken Finn is a different matter entirely. I say "young," because he may be only 14. If you say to him, "What the hell are you staring at?" you have created a potentially dangerous situation. First, he will probably understand you. Second, if he is young enough, drunk enough, and big enough, he may flatten your face, thus requiring extensive, and expensive, plastic surgery.

A young Finn loaded with vodka is an extremely dangerous creature. And the country seems to be full of them. I don't know why this is true; normally, Finland is a very safe and orderly country. But their young drunkards are to be carefully avoided.

The Arctic cold certainly hasn't chilled the Finnish blood. The people are extremely friendly (especially when they've been drinking) and seem to like Americans. A group at the bar and restaurant where I was having dinner in Rovaniemi beckoned me to join them. Since one of them was an incredibly gorgeous blonde (she looked like she had just returned victorious from the Miss America contest), I hastened to comply.

Sadly, her English was limited to "ya" and "danka," but she seemed interested in me. I told her I was entirely too old for an extremely vigorous-looking Finnish maiden, but she didn't understand a word. Neither did anybody else in the place; they just smiled a lot.

There was only one problem. Like everyone else in Finland over the age of 12, she was never without a cigarette in her lovely mouth. Her breath smelled like a cross between a barnyard and a spittoon — wreeecht! I tried to hold my breath a lot.

Something's missing at Christmas

My mission on this trip to Finland was not only to pull myself back from starvation, but to find a place to live when my Russian sojourn ends. Since I was still exploring many scientific and business possibilities with photoluminescence, I wanted to be close enough to St. Petersburg to return easily. Finland seemed ideal.

But this trip almost caused me to change my mind. It's the "Christmas" season in Finland and everywhere you look, there are the usual tacky displays for that pre-Leninist do-gooder, Santa Claus (or Father Frost, as he's known in these parts).

I put Christmas in quotes in the paragraph above, because this winter festival in Finland has nothing to do with the birth of Christ. I didn't see a SINGLE REFERENCE to the Christian meaning of December 25 in the whole city of Helsinki. It's actually more like Easter, only they resurrect Bing Crosby ("I'm dreaming of ..."), rather than the Son of God. I wonder what the Finns celebrate at Easter. Probably a festival for an egg-laying bunny rabbit, just like at home.

At least there's one improvement in Finland: Their television doesn't run ten commercials an hour for "the amazing Salad Shooter."

Now, don't misunderstand me; I LIKE Finland. If you are unhappy in this secular world, then you'll just have to wait for happiness in the next, because this one isn't going to change.

Nabbed by the police

The next day, I stopped by a bank in downtown Helsinki, to pick up some money that had been wired from the States. As I turned away from the teller's window, having said the requisite "keetose" to the nice lady who took care of me, two husky Finnish police officers accosted me. While the bank clerks looked on in wide-eyed shock (I had seemed so nice, they seemed to be saying to themselves), the police demanded to see my passport and then escorted me out of the building.

I was very politely, but very firmly, hustled into an antiseptically clean Nissan police car and off we sped. After a few minutes we pulled up to an unmarked building with an automatic steel door. This is looking REALLY bad, I thought. What had I done to arouse the ire of their equivalent of the FBI? Had I spit on the sidewalk? No. Had I jaywalked? Well, yes, but that was yesterday.

They sat me down at a bench and about a dozen of Helsinki's finest something-or-other studied my passport and occasionally glanced over at me, not malevolently, you understand, but with a detached interest as if I were some sort of bug under a glass.

I thought, "My passport — THAT'S it. It's all those Russian customs stamps." The Finns don't like Russians very much; they remember a hundred years of czarist occupation and the Winter War as if they happened yesterday.

Then my imagination began to overheat: Somebody in Russia has framed me. I'm going to be the fall guy for a big smuggling operation. I was about to demand to see my lawyer (who was 5,000 miles away) when a pleasant fellow came over from the group and said: "There has been a mistake. Come into my office and I will explain."

It seems there was a foreigner loose up in the wilds of northern Finland who called himself an Indian and was going to teach the Finns all about saving their country from industrial purgatory. The Finns like their country just the way it is and, being nature-lovers without parallel, they don't think they need the advice of some environmentalist kook from Kukamonga.

As I was obviously a foreigner, they had to bring me in for questioning. At least that's what the nice man said; it didn't seem that "obvious" to me. I hadn't been muttering to myself, accosting their citizens, or arguing politics. Heck, I don't even *look* like an Indian. Then I decided: It must be my hat! I was wearing my Indiana Jones special — that must have been it. I wasn't really concerned anyway; I knew their jails would be clean and comfortable.

"So, we apologize for the error," he said cheerily. "Where would you like for us to take you?"

"Well, I think it would be nice if your boys took me back to the bank and explained to the ladies that I'm not a criminal. I don't want to be faced with Uzis the next time I go in for money."

He agreed that was an excellent idea. The police officer and I went into the bank together and he explained in Finnish that I really was a nice man, just as they had thought. At least I think that's what he said.

Stopped at customs

The contrasts between western Russia and Finland, two countries that are juxtaposed and topographically look the same, are remarkable. It just shows how one insane socialist with a genius for organization (Lenin may have been a fruitcake otherwise, but he was an organizer and manipulator of Machiavellian proportions) can destroy the lives of millions and a century of magnificent culture.

You walk into a bus terminal or railway station in Russia and you are in a zoo. The door crashes behind you as in a prison; you're surrounded by trash, spittle, and the smell of urine. Don't even THINK of visiting the toilets — they are dirtier than those in the hospitals. The smoke is so thick in the waiting room that you can hardly read the "No Smoking!" sign on the opposite wall.

Some sophisticated travelers tell me, "You just have to put up with a little dirt when you travel in the Third World. That's part of the ambience of the thing." I have traveled the world over and I DO put up with it. But I still prefer my ambience CLEAN when I can get it.

I was checking out accommodations in Turku, Finland (on the west coast, an hour's easy train ride from Helsinki) and walked into the terminal and ticketing office of the Viking Line. It was like entering a surgical suite of an American hospital. It didn't have the "ambience" of scruffy Russia, but clean is also nice, don't you think?

Traveling by bus from Finland back to Russia brought a strange sense of *deja vu* to me. It was similar to traveling from San Diego to Tijuana, Mexico. You go from orderliness, cleanliness, well-paved roads, and efficient bureaucracy, to chaos, filth, pot holes, trash, and a sullen, inefficient bureaucracy.

When I passed through customs on my way to Finland, I declared 4,000 rubles on the form: it was a rough estimate of what I had in my pocket. On the way back, a week later, I'd forgotten what I'd said earlier and declared that I had 7,000 rubles. The difference didn't seem important to me, but the massive and decidedly unfriendly Russian gorgon behind the customs counter acted as though I belonged on their "most wanted" list.

Epaulets shaking on her fancy uniform (Russians *love* uniforms and think they should be *de rigueur* for every occupation), she thundered: "Why did you take 4,000 rubles out of Russia? Where did you get the other 3,000 you are bringing back in? Don't you know it's illegal to take rubles in and out of Russia?"

An entire busload of impatient people was being held up by one suspected felon — me. I felt a little panic as I actually had something like 20,000 rubles in my possession. I was afraid we were reaching the stage of a personal search. I excused myself to go to the bathroom. I'm surprised she let me go, but maybe she took pride that she'd made me nervous enough to require a pit stop.

Once in the john, I wasn't sure what to do. I didn't want to flush my rubles and I wasn't sure I could, even if I were willing to sacrifice them. As is customary in any public facility in Russia, the toilet was broken and full of you-know-what. I thought of swallowing them, but that wasn't very appealing, either.

I have never seen the inside of a Russian jail, but I figure they've *got* to be worse than their hospitals. That thought was enough to terrify me. What to do, what to do. I ended up stashing most of the rubles in my boot. Hey, I know it's not the cleverest ploy you've ever heard, but it was all I could think of at the time.

Fortunately, customs officials in Russia are prone to be quite stupid. They didn't question my trip to the toilet, so I decided the best defense was to go on the offense. I would portray outraged innocence and indignation. After a heated exchange that neither side understood (probably fortunately for me), she shoved my passport at me, including, to my surprise, the hot rubles.

You may be wondering how much money we were talking about in this "international crisis." The difference between 7,000 rubles and 4,000 rubles, at that time, was around seven dollars. Only in Russia would that be enough to make me a dangerous international criminal.

A monument to socialist failure

The train ride from the Finnish border to St. Petersburg is one of the most depressing rides on earth. You've left clean, fresh, sparkling, friendly Helsinki. You're going back to filthy, unsanitary, polluted Russia. And the very first town you come to after you cross the border is Vieborg, an industrial corpse. The factories are empty, smokeless, on permanent holiday.

One abandoned brick building in particular caught my eye as we bumped and rattled our way past. Printed in raised brick on the wall facing the train is the date "1954." No doubt it was put there to commemorate the opening of the factory. I'm sure that at the dedication ceremonies, they emptied a few bottles of vodka in celebration of another step toward "building socialism."

It's been 40 years. The dictator with the unpronounceable name who called himself Stalin died the year before the factory was completed — long live the new father of the people, Nikita Khrushchev.

Forty years later the factory has open spaces, like the sockets of a human skull, where once there had been windows. In its shroud of rain-soaked weeds it proclaims: Failure, Failure, Failure. It is an appropriate monument to the Great October Socialist Revolution.

There is a bright side to the failure of socialist industry in Vieborg: the air is clean and the people can breathe again. They don't have much to eat, but they can breathe.

I'm sure the citizens of Vieborg would much prefer to see the smoke again. It would mean the return of sausage, borscht with real meat, and (one can dream, can't one?) maybe even asparagus, something that's been unknown to Russians for generations.

And so, back to St. Pete.

Chapter Fourteen

The Mighty Soviet Army
and Other Popular Myths

You've got to see it to believe it: Soviet Army Day. That's the day the government pretends that their army is the best darn army that ever existed and without it, Mother Russia would have long ago succumbed to the capitalist oppressors of the West — and the Nazis before that. But if you look beyond the propaganda, it is quickly apparent that the Russian army (and the Soviet army before it) isn't worth a damn.

The Soviet army didn't win World War II, either. They had some great and much-publicized victories, such as Stalingrad and the 900-day siege of Leningrad, true. But without our help, and Hitler's bungling, today they would be playing "Deutschland Uber Alles" on the loudspeakers rather than "From the Taiga to the British Sea — the Red Army Is the Strongest of All!"

Did you know that a large portion of the Red Army tried to surrender to the Nazis, and wanted nothing more than to turn around and liberate their country from the communists? Hitler was too suspicious to realize he was being handed a historic opportunity and put them all in prison camps.

The army of imperial Russia under Czar Nicholas II acquitted itself very well and held the Germans off for most of World War I. The army was disciplined and had excellent generalship, especially that of Lieutenant General Gustof

Mannerheim, the Finn who later defended his homeland against the Red Army. But after the Bolsheviks took over and murdered some of Russia's best generals (Mannerheim barely escaped), the army quickly degenerated into a mob of drunken thieves and rapists who couldn't put down an insurrection in a retirement home.

During World War I, the soldiers at the front (newly "communized" and leaderless) simply quit fighting. The Germans could have moved into Moscow with little or no resistance. By the fall of 1917, the Russian army had virtually ceased to exist. Lenin, realizing the drunken mob called the Red Army was worthless, made a halfhearted attempt to mobilize the sailors, who had always been more zealous in the communist cause than the army, and sent them to the front to fight the Germans. But by then their revolutionary zeal had also dimmed and, instead of attacking the Germans, they raided the distilleries, grabbed all the booze, and chased women.

Realizing they would have to start from scratch to build a military force, and not trusting the reeling mob that was the remainder of the czarist army, some of the communist leaders proposed a program to "arm everyone." Wiser heads in the dictatorial regime realized, however, that arming the entire populace could spell *finis* to their own exalted persons, once the peasants realized how they had been deceived. So instead of arming everyone, they introduced iron-fisted anti-gun laws — just like New York City enjoys today.

Back to the Germans and World War I. Lenin had no real intention of resisting his benefactors, and after some pretended belligerence, ("The socialist fatherland is in danger!"), he ordered a complete capitulation to every German demand. Russia ceded to Germany all of the territory its troops occupied. Lenin also promised massive indemnity — which was paid in full IN GOLD.

This complete and unconditional surrender to Germany took place on February 23, 1918. Nonetheless, this date was chosen as the day of annual celebration of the glorious accomplishments of the Red Army. Talk about rewriting history!

Russian home, vintage 18th century. (I'm a little younger.)

(Once again, let me thank my guardian seagull,
Dr. Nikolai Chaika, who took all the photographs in this section and
did so much else to help me — WCD)

Winter 1992.
It was cold, *very* cold.

Waiting for my CIA contact. Volodga, 1992

Some people will do *anything* to avoid the boredom of socialism!

Novgorod, 1992. More like the 14th century than 20th — or even the 18th. It's amazing so little has changed in the last 500 years.

My triumphal return after a fattening-up trip to Finland.
(Lenin is still there — he is everywhere in Russia.)

Low point, Christmas '92. But at least I had a tree.

Nikolai, Leda, and "Beel." I smiled more whenever I was
with them.

Telephones are a problem
— they don't work. Below, a
typical street band.

Mrs. Nikolai Chaika ("Galia")

Escape to the forest — will Spring ever come?

Eighty percent of the churches were destroyed by the communists, but plenty remain.

Many are truly spectacular; some plain. But all of them have a story to tell.

The old stock exchange of tzarist times.
Vasilefsky Point, St. Petersburg, 1992.

There are *a lot more* where this came from. Novgorod, Russia.

The Winter Palace in St. Petersburg.

I still don't look like a native, do I?

Treasures from centuries past.

Nikolai didn't take *all* the pictures — this is my best shot.

Spring in St. Petersburg, 1992. Rain, rain, go away.

On Nevsky Prospekt, Spring 1993, with Leda, my lubemaya.

Going home soon —
mixed emotions.

As more people learn the truth about the history of their glorious army, the celebration of this day of ignominious defeat is an uncomfortable reminder of the insanity of it all. So, this year, Russia's rulers changed the holiday from Soviet Army Day to Defenders of the Fatherland Day.

By the way, the glorious Red navy isn't faring any better today than the army. I've seen reports that four navy cadets at a base in the far east actually starved to death. Another 86 were hospitalized for malnutrition.

As the navy is in such a deplorable state, bits and pieces of it are being offered for sale. You can pick up a formerly top-secret Piranha-class submarine that has never been wet for less than $10 million and start your own little empire. But a word of warning: Russian submarines sometimes rise back to the surface, and sometimes they don't. Before taking your first dive in your shiny new toy, check out the resurfacing mechanism, the toilets, the sinks, and the integrity of the bathtub drain and stopper. The deal is cash on delivery, in dollars, no warranty.

Needed: an economic miracle

The country is imploding economically; there's no doubt about that. The Russian pouchta (post office), for example, has completely collapsed as far as outgoing mail is concerned. You can't mail a letter out of Russia because most of the time, *there are no stamps*. Even if there were stamps, your letter would likely never leave the country. I have had air mail packages take THREE MONTHS to reach me. Adding insult to injury, they often arrive in a pulverized condition, as a result of an "inspection." Oh, you have to pay extra for the "inspection," too. If you don't cough up this not-so-subtle bribe, your package will never reach you.

It's unrealistic to think Russia can have any semblance of "democracy" under the present circumstances. Few people alive today in Russia have ever experienced any freedom and most of them don't want it. I have pretty much concluded that the only thing that will rescue Russia from the cataclysm is a military dictatorship.

Yes, I mean what I said above: The majority of Russians don't want freedom. In a recent survey, 51 percent said they believed authoritarian rule was the best solution for their country; only 31 percent preferred democracy. That result isn't surprising; Russians have always been told what to do, where to go, what to think, and whom to hate.

Now that Russians know they have been lied to for 70 years, and that they, not American workers, were the ones being exploited, how can they be expected to have any faith in their leaders? After 200 years of freedom in the United States, we're producing some of the most despicable politicians who have ever disgraced this planet; how can we expect the Russians to do in one generation what we haven't been able to achieve in a century?

No wonder there is a growing radicalism among the youth of Russia. Their emotions and gullibility are being exploited by the right wing, which in Russia means the militarists and the communists. One of the most popular new groups is something called the Russian National Council; the name sounds innocuous enough, but it's run by the "former" KGB general, Alexander Sterligov, a *very* dangerous man.

Another worrisome organization appealing to young Russians is Pamyat. This group has been armed, probably by the "former" KGB, in case they are needed in the fight against "Jewish freemasons" and "agents of world imperialism." It's hard to tell from the rhetoric whether they are Nazis or communists, but there never was much difference anyway.

If Russia were fortunate enough to have a military leader like Chile's Augustine Pinochet take power, a military dictatorship could be a very good thing. It will take an incredibly strong ruler to clean out the nomenklatur, the mafia, and the bureaucracy, and tell the people: "You're going to have a market-based, capitalistic economy, whether you want one or not. You will have to work hard, but your labors will be rewarded, because the state is not going to take from you what you have honestly earned. There will be a reasonable tax on your earnings, and you will be given tax incentives to invest your money in the Russian economy. In effect, the more you earn, the lower your tax rate will be. People caught stealing and manipulating the economy for their own personal gain will be severely punished."

A Russian would understand that approach. At first he wouldn't believe it, but he'd understand it. This is probably pure fantasy on my part, but the economic miracles in Chile, Taiwan, Singapore, Japan, Hong Kong, Korea, and other places prove what can be done when the free market is allowed to perform its wonders.

Guarding a wax dummy

Speaking of wonders, it's gotten a little embarrassing to see the hourly ritual at Lenin's tomb where the guard is changed with such great fanfare and solemnity. People are snickering, "When are they going to close down that silly wax museum?" (Of course it's a wax dummy. You didn't really believe those stories that the Russians had devised a system to preserve a corpse for 70 years, did you?)

A handful of Russian deputies has actually begun to question the appropriateness of honoring the man who created a regime that is so universally despised. It would be like Americans having a tomb and guard of honor, changed every four hours around the clock, for King George the Third. Or better yet, for Benedict Arnold.

The dozen or so deputies who want to get rid of this vile reminder of the recent past said in a letter addressed to President Yeltsin: "The guards are a challenge to the memory of millions of victims of the Lenin regime and point to the lack of firmness in our government in view of the increasingly offensive behavior of the proponents of the totalitarian past."

I predict the wax statue reclining so elegantly in its open coffin will soon be removed and given "a decent burial" in some secret place — unless the commies take over again.

Late news: Just recently, Lenin's "mummy house" was closed and the fancy honor guard stopped showing up. The tomb will make a nice Baskin-Robbins outlet.

An idyllic afternoon

Greta and I spent last Sunday at Tzarsko Selo, the palace in Pushkin, about a half-hour south of St. Petersburg. Pushkin is not far from Pulkava Hill, where Hitler's troops looked longingly at the city they couldn't conquer.

The palace there is one of the most magnificent in all of Russia. The Nazis pulverized it, not because it had any military significance, but merely as a way to demoralize the people. The restoration of Tzarsko Selo has been remarkable, as is the restoration of so much else the Nazis destroyed. Russian craftsmen can do extraordinary things with wood, paint, and stone. Why can't they do as well with steel and electricity and get the elevators to work? It's another paradox in a country that is filled with them.

Greta was quite fetching in her tight jeans and short-sleeved blouse. Her long, slender legs didn't hurt the overall effect, either. We were rushing spring a bit, as the weather was chilly and damp. But we had real coffee, which I had purchased at the Hotel Europe, as well as some Western goodies from the hard currency store. Our picnic was expensive, but worth it.

Greta told me about her family, her boyfriend in Sweden, the usual stuff. We talked about Russia and its chances of achieving the good life. We agreed that the prospects were not good. We also talked about the election of the Clintons. Neither of us was very happy about that. Greta wondered how much longer *we* would have the good life, with the Clintons "reinventing" the socialist state.

The day passed all too quickly. I really enjoyed it. We made tentative plans to go to the opera. I said I would call her once I had the tickets.

Goodbye, dear Greta

I won't be seeing Greta anymore. When I called her about the opera, she said, "Bill, I have a problem." Uh, oh. "I won't be able to see you again." Double uh, oh.

I was stunned. I thought we had enjoyed a *great* relationship. We had fun together; we relieved each other's boredom; we even thought the same politically. Once, as we were observing a Soviet bus puffing along and listing dangerously to starboard, she blurted out, "Too bad Hitler didn't win the war. Things would at least work here." No Nazi, this girl, not even close. She just saw things as they were — amazing for 21.

"Why can't you see me? What's happened? Did I say something that offended you? I have these great tickets...."

"Bill," she interrupted, "you know I have a boyfriend in Sweden...."

"Yes, of course. We've discussed it."

"Well, he phoned last night and I told him about you, that we were just hanging out, going to concerts, doing a little cross-country skiing — but not overnight or anything. [*That's* the part she should have left out.] He just didn't feel comfortable with the concept — do you understand?"

"Yes," I lied, "but did you tell him I'm old enough to be your father? That in fact I'm *older* than your father?"

"I told him that, but it didn't help."

"Why not," I asked.

"Because *he's* old enough to be my father!"

Now I understood. I'll make other friends, so it doesn't matter.

Who am I kidding? Of *course* it matters. I'll miss that 40-year-old brain in a pretty 21-year-old head. Guess I can't blame him.

Chapter Fifteen

The Bus to Novgorod

You've probably never heard of Novgorod. I hadn't before moving to St. Petersburg, yet it's one of Russia's oldest cities, with some marvelous examples of 14th century architecture that have been preserved virtually intact. I'd wanted to see it ever since I'd heard about it, so Nikolia and I finally made the trip there last week.

For some reason no one could explain to me, the Bolsheviks didn't destroy all the churches in this ancient city. Those that were destroyed are being carefully rebuilt and restored. If you overlook all the ugly communist architectural overlay, it was like stepping back into the 14th century. No matter what your religion, or even if you don't have one, these ancient masterpieces will fill you with an admiration for the eternal search for God that man elicits in the face of seemingly insurmountable obstacles.

The Russian church in the mid-20th century had two enemies determined to destroy it. What the communists didn't manage to obliterate prior to 1941, the Nazis attempted to destroy. Yet, there is Novgorod with its dozens of churches declaring that God is not dead.

Even though I had grown used to the backwardness of Russian life, I was startled to see women in the middle of this city of 250,000 drawing water for their homes from a common well (in the snow and -4 degree weather). The old pump with its black metal arm looked no different from the one my great-grandmother Lucy used in the Georgia mountains a hundred years ago. (The privies looked the same, too.)

Typhoid fever has almost disappeared in the advanced countries of the world. I have never seen a case in 30 years of practice in the U.S. But typhoid is rampant in Russia and its former satellites. And no wonder, in virtually all of the villages and even many of the larger towns, such as Vologda and Novgorod, you'll find outside privies in the center of town.

The combination of hundreds of privies near the community water supplies is an open invitation to typhoid and cholera. A highly placed expert on Russian public health told me that probably 95 percent of the people in these towns have been or are infected with typhoid fever. Most of the cases go undiagnosed and untreated. Most recover with no medical therapy (the Russians are tough), and then have lifetime immunity.

Living like a millionaire

I decided to treat my travelling companions to a meal at the best restaurant in town. We were guided to an ancient tower in the Novgorod kremlin, where we listened to an excellent and enthusiastic Russian folk band, had a bottle of the local firewater specialty (served with a liquid fruit compote to keep it from dissolving our esophagus), and enjoyed a great borsch, salad, and dessert. (Our serving girl had light yellow, almost platinum, hair. I thought she was lovely; she never noticed me.)

The bill for three of us came to $6. I paid it cheerfully, but Nikolai was concerned about my spending so much money. (You have to keep in mind that my $6 extravagance represented *a full week's pay* for him.)

The total cost for our two-day trip, including meals, lodging, and bus fare for three of us, came to $25. It would have been $19, but the hotel jacked up our bill an extra $1 a night for each of us, just so they could sock it to the rich American. I looked grumpy and sour when I paid it; I always do that, so they won't think they've really put one over on me. They'd be horribly insulted if they realized what was a small fortune to them is only pocket change to many of us.

For the first time in my life I know what it is like to feel like a millionaire. I'm sure that when you are a millionaire, everything under $100 seems almost free. You just don't think about such trivial sums.

Well, in Russia, where you pay $6 for a first class round-trip ticket from St. Petersburg to Moscow (and that's for a compartment for four), $1.50 for dinner, less than a penny for a subway ride, eight cents for a bottle of beer, or two cents for a roll of black and white film, you stop paying attention to the price — for you, it's almost free.

You can't explain that to Nikolai, though. And you can't tell him that, when you return to the West, where one night in a first-class hotel can cost *more* than a month's rent in St. Petersburg, you immediately suffer a near-terminal case of sticker shock.

A good, brisk dip

The next morning in Novgorod, while walking along the banks of the river that flows through the town, I was astounded to see a young girl in an ill-fitting bikini (ill-fitting because there was too much girl and not enough bikini) casually walking barefoot down the opposite snow-covered river bank and out onto the frozen river.

Fifty yards or so onto the ice, she came to a hole about the size of a manhole cover with a ladder protruding from it. She casually tossed her towel aside and climbed into the water. (The ambient temperature was three degrees below freezing. When we got back to the hotel, I checked.)

The woman remained in the water for a minute or two, dog-paddling around in circles. She then climbed out, picked up her towel, and strolled back up the embankment.

"Nikolai," I said, "that was the strangest thing I have ever seen."

"Yes, Beel, it was strange," Nikolai acknowledged. "One does not go swimming in the ice holes alone. What's more," he added thoughtfully, "she was not wearing shoes. Very strange."

I told you these Russians are tough.

A place in the country

We left Novgorod in a blinding snowstorm with a bus driver who looked suspiciously drunk. "Do you think he's a drunkard, Nikolai?" I asked.

"Of COURSE he's a drunkard, Beel," he replied with the intonation that I shouldn't bother him with such foolish questions. I reached for my non-existent seatbelt.

We passed dozens of little villages on the way back to St. Petersburg. Before the Great October Socialist Revolution, all of these villages had at least one church, and sometimes two. In the 150-kilometer trip, I saw only one church. The rest had been destroyed by decree of the great democrat, Vladimir Illyich Lenin.

But one thing I did see were hundreds of "summer houses." If you travel anywhere in Russia outside the larger cities, you will see clusters of these tiny houses, little more than huts. There is no evidence of a commercial support system nearby — no stores, no street lamps, no office buildings, just hundreds of little shacks no bigger than your living room, huddled together like frightened ugly ducklings.

These are not villages, but "summer houses" where the Russian can get away from the city and have all the inconveniences of being near the Russian earth they love so much: dirt, mud (LOTS of mud), dampness, and a penetrating cold.

When I first arrived in Russia, I repeatedly heard people proudly referring to their summer house. How is it possible, I thought, for people who are so destitute they have to live in high-rise dog kennels provided by the state, and make a wage considered substandard in China, to afford a "summer house"?

The summer house, I soon learned, was little more than a cow shed constructed of waste lumber, discarded auto or truck carcasses, scraps of plywood, and anything else that didn't turn to mush in the rain.

The government doles out tiny plots of land in the hinterlands for the building of these precious refuges from the city. They have no plumbing, no lights, no heat, and no refrigeration. They are damp and cold in the winter and damp and hot in the summer. Plus, the summer brings the added companionship of millions of flies and mosquitoes.

Russians think their shacks are absolutely wonderful. They make life worth living ... for a Russian.

It's in their blood

Russians have a very romantic attraction to the soil and anything Russian. The Russian soil is such a magnetic influence that they are willing to sacrifice all their free time working on their summer home and growing a few potatoes and cucumbers. It often becomes an obsession that occupies them winter and summer.

In the last analysis, Russians aren't Marxists and they aren't monarchists — and they certainly aren't democrats. I think perhaps in their heart of hearts they are really peasants. But they are always and forevermore *Russian*.

Ironically, this adoration of the Russian soil was not shared by the muzhiks who were tied to it, by circumstance or serfdom, before the industrial revolution. They were forced into communes long before the word communism was known; they had absolutely no legal recourse from a cruel or extorting master, as lodging complaints was prohibited and, anyway, they were not permitted to appear in court. They could be forced into marriage to a partner chosen by the lord of the manor. And the master could, and often did, cull the prettiest serf girls for his personal harem.

The Great Russian Soil was a repugnant and despicable glue to the peasant who would go to almost any means, including murder and a life of uncertain vagabondage, to escape it. The only thing that held him in check was his attachment to his family and the fear of a beating or hanging if caught.

About once every 100 years, the frustrations of the peasant would boil over and he would go on a rampage, killing landlords and tax collectors and burning everything in sight. Professor Richard Pipes, an American historian and expert in Russian history, recognized this truism when he wrote,

> There is no evidence that the Russian peasant loved the soil; this sentiment is to be found mainly in the imagination of gentry romantics who visit their estates in the summer time.

This sentimental adoration of the Russian soil persists today in the summer-house obsession. The city folk, only one generation removed from peasant life, have never shaken off many aspects of their peasant background.

There is one charming old farm custom that persists to this day: if you visit a family in the city, you will almost certainly be given a jar of homemade preserves when you leave. In the spring and summer, the city empties and every single mushroom and wild berry for miles around is picked and then canned so they can honor visitors with their small gift.

I originally decided to award the Novgorod hotel two garlic buds on my personal rating guide. At first it was going to be one-and-a-half, but my room contained a radio. It didn't work, but the thought earned them half a garlic.

On arriving back to St. Petersburg and semi-civilization, I had Trotsky's Trot for three days, requiring copious amounts of Rossiyskaya vodka. I blamed it on the water in Novgorod and cut their rating to one garlic bud.

Another disadvantage to the hotel in Novgorod was that the acoustics were not exactly studio quality. I could hear the young couple next door having sex every morning and night. (I don't know about noon because I wasn't there at lunchtime.)

I was amazed, because I had never heard of such Russian enthusiasm for sex. What with all the alcohol they consume, I didn't think Russian men could be that active.

Turns out the couple was Polish.

Chapter Sixteen

Russia's Remarkable Women

Of all the meaningless holidays in Russia (Red Army Day, Day of the Revolution, you name it), the most hypocritical is "International Women's Day," when the women are to have a blessed day of rest from their ceaseless toil. The way it usually works is that it is the MEN who take the day off. The boys spend the day down at the bar instead of at work. But they will have left a few wilting carnations at home, along with a card declaiming that their female colleague is "the most charming and alluring" partner in the world. What more could a woman want?

When a Russian woman does get the day off, she uses it to catch up on the housework which, of course, is too complicated for her drunken husband. If he's home, he will lounge in a chair and look longingly at the kitchen, wondering if Women's Day means he won't get fed.

Lenin's wife, Krupskaya, who looked remarkably like a codfish, prophesied that the Soviet Union would be the first society in which women would be liberated and truly free. What Russian women got instead is a brutish and drunken lout who can't do anything for himself and thinks his wife should be a combination mother, whore, and housekeeper. She's often the breadwinner as well.

There's a joke that's a great favorite with Russia's over-worked, under-appreciated, and unloved women: A husband says to his wife, "Darling, it's March 8, what is your greatest desire?"

Her eyes light up. "Boris, make me really happy — promise not to sleep with me tonight!"

Seventy-five years after the Great October Socialist Revolution, the communists' much-heralded New Man has failed to arrive. What poor Natasha has is the old variety who gets drunk on her day off, has no idea how to work the stove, and thinks that three carnations and a box of cheap imitation chocolates will make up for his shortcomings.

There is no doubt that Russian women are the stronger sex. Much of the time, they treat the men in their life like babies. On the subway you will often see a woman cradling her intoxicated son or husband as you would a child. It is a depressing sight and one hopes that Russia will someday produce the incredibly strong and brave Russian man of old. But I'm not optimistic.

A friend of mine related the pathetic story of his mother-in-law. She is 80 years old and lives in a tiny room with no bathroom. The bathroom is in a separate building 200 yards down the street. (Remember, it hits 40 degrees below zero here.) But she is lucky. Many of these old people, some hardly able to walk, have to trudge a half mile on dangerously slippery, icy streets to reach this public bathroom.

Having a bathroom in your flat is often only a little better. Some apartments are so crowded that the occupants have to stand in line in the morning to go to the toilet.

As I've mentioned before, pensioners (again, most of them women) also stand in line every month at the post office to collect a little stack of coins as their month's livelihood. They get about 2,000 rubles a month (the Russian currency is pronounced, appropriately enough, as "rubbles"). Thirty years ago, the ruble was worth 25 cents; today, thanks to massive inflation in Russia, it is worth 3/10s of a cent.

So on the equivalent of six dollars a month, these old, anemic retirees (virtually all of them suffer from nutritional anemia and are in a state of semi-starvation) are expected to eke out an existence.

In this desperate state, they will try anything to augment their pittance in order to get enough food for the month. A typical scene at the street market: An old and bent babushka purchases half a kilogram of potatoes. She pays, walks a few feet away, then rushes back to the vendor, claiming he gave her only half of the full kilo of potatoes she paid for. The seller shows no mercy and she departs disappointed.

These pitiful old people are not dishonest, they are desperate. They are the mothers and fathers of the present working generation — children who don't have the room in their overcrowded flat, or the money to take care of their aging parents. The pensioners know their raise next month will not be enough to cover the inflation rate, which is currently running about one percent per day.

Even more depressing than the old peasant women scrambling for survival are the many young-to-middle-aged women of obvious breeding and class standing on street corners, offering to sell a book or lamp or some other household article. Often they are wearing fur coats they hope they won't have to sell for food to feed their family. These women bother me more, I think, because they once had a good life and lost it. The old peasant women never had it much better than they do now.

Stealing "the people's" wood

I went to the forest north of St. Petersburg over the weekend with some Russian friends. There was some snow, but most of it had turned into that famous Russian mud, the kind that defeated Napoleon and Hitler.

Walking down a road of this black mud, we encountered an old woman gathering wood. She looked at us with suspicion and mistrust. Why were we there? What did we want? Would we tell the authorities about her? It is illegal, you see, for her to gather wood in the forest. It is true that there is plenty of wood, and that she needs the wood for cooking and heating her home. But the *state* owns all the property (including her hut) and it is a crime to take any of the wood owned by the people.

What should she do? She should buy her wood at the state stores that have been generously set up for the people's use. The nearest one is probably only a few miles away; let her walk!

But it is impossible to find wood at the state stores and, anyway, how can an old woman haul wood on her back, even if it is available, for miles back to her izba?

So naturally, she "steals" the wood from the forest. If she is caught, she will give the forester a bottle of vodka to avoid being arrested and sent to jail. It sometimes seems that in Russia, everyone is forced to become a liar and a thief to survive.

Another example of the merciless exploitation of women is the pathetic story of Ananastasia Maxima.

Ananastasia devoted her life to the diamond mines in the frozen wastes of Siberia, which has some of the worst weather in the world. In winter, the temperature will often settle in at -40 degrees. Ananastasia was a dedicated Communist when she volunteered 35 years ago to help "build socialism" in the diamond mines of nature's deep freeze. convict labor is used in other types of mining, where the workers are simply worked to death, but diamonds were so important to the national economy that only dedicated Communist Party members and members of the Communist Youth League were allowed to suffer in the Siberian diamond industry.

These patriots and idealists, who had swallowed the party line whole, were told their "glorious labor" in the mines was to supply industrial diamonds for the people's industry. They knew nothing of diamonds or their worth. They had been reviled for years about the evil South Africans and their slave-owning company, DeBeers, that exploited blacks and used the sweat of their labor to adorn wealthy capitalist women of the West with their dirty diamonds. In Russia, they were told, diamonds were only used as a cutting agent to build the Soviet industrial might in order to bring down the capitalist West.

Only recently have they found out that their government has been working hand-in-glove with DeBeers all along. Workers, like Ananastasia, spent their entire lives working for the very enemy the government was telling them they were fighting — at

$52 a month. Trying to hide her shame and sense of hopelessness, Ananastasia shrugs her shoulders: "This is Russia."

The First Lady of Russia

One contemporary female who is definitely NOT your average Russian woman is Raisa Gorbachev, wife of the former Kremlin ruler and now candidate for President of the World. (Mark my words: You haven't heard the last of him.)

Raisa Gorbachev, who became a star of our slick magazine industry, rose effortlessly to the status of Russia's most hated woman by wielding her Kremlin American Express card with gusto on every foreign trip.

Raisa is Russia's most boring woman. In the time it takes her to say one sentence, you could go to the kitchen, make a sandwich, swallow it, *and* drink a cold beer, then go to the bathroom and brush you teeth.

"I think ... that ..." (you've made your sandwich) "there is ..." (you've eaten it) "a possibility ..." (your teeth are now clean — and on edge) "that ..." (you fall into an ennui-induced coma and are arrested for your lack of respect to the wife of the former president of all the Russias).

Gorby with his childish, simplistic Russian and Raisa with her sloth-like Russian are one heck of a pair. How do boorish turtleheads like this get into power, anyway?

Finally, I meet my Lara

By Christmas time, I was finally getting comfortable with my quasi-solitary life. I had survived the food, the mosquitoes, the second thoughts, the dreams of home. I had adapted. But when you're alone, walking the streets of a city, you notice that most people are in pairs. This constantly reminds you that no matter how well-adjusted you feel, you're only half the picture. And if there's no one with whom you can share your excitement, that excitement is somehow diminished.

I was invited to attend a performance at the Philharmonic Jazz Hall, a doughty former movie theatre where the seats had been removed and replaced with tables. It's a great place to just hang out and have a cold peva while listening to some of the best jazz in the world. The musicians are Russian, but the music is decidedly American.

A strikingly attractive woman sat down at the table next to us. She was unaccompanied, so I invited her to join our group. Apparently we seemed harmless enough, because she agreed.

Her name is Leda. And she is not only beautiful (she looks like Anne Archer), but quite intelligent, too. She has a slow, bubbling laugh and a warm and captivating personality. She's the kind of woman every man dreams about (or at least this one does).

During the intermission, Leda asked me about my life in the city and what I did. I explained that I was doing research at various hospitals and wrote a lot when at my apartment because, not speaking the language, I didn't have many friends.

"It must be lonely for you, Beel," she replied.

"Well, yes. What I need is some beautiful lady like you to talk with. But I would undoubtedly fall in love with you — I'm far too old for you and so I would have to endure the pain of our separation, which would be bound to happen. You see, I'm trying to avoid any more pain in my life. Will you have dinner with me tomorrow night?"

"No, Beel."

Well okay, that's that, I thought. I was stupid to rush things. I should have maintained my cool, as the kids would say.

"Perhaps next week," she said, and my heart started beating again.

We exchanged phone numbers and made plans to meet on Sunday afternoon. After the show, I walked her to the subway. When it came time to part, I wanted to throw her over my shoulder and carry her back to my apartment. Instead, I kissed her hand and wished her good night.

As I made my way back to my flat, I said to myself, she can't be THAT beautiful, THAT intelligent, THAT charming. Almost everybody looks better in dim light. Maybe it was the vodka; maybe it was just my solitary lifestyle catching up with me.

We agreed to meet on Sunday at Dom Kinige, a popular bookstore on Nevsky Prospekt. That was a long time away — three whole days. Why, I'd be three days older by then.

Chapter Seventeen

The Joy of Sects

Contrary to popular belief, using the church as an arm of the government didn't start with the communists; it's been a time-honored tradition for generations here in Mother Russia. In fact, the government minister of the church was usually a general of the army.

The average Russian (if there is such a thing) is not fooled by the hypocrisy of the Russian Orthodox Church. It was hardly a secret that the priests reported to the Okrana during the czarist years and were paid by the czarist government. If a heresy appeared, the priests only had to report it to the authorities and the security forces would quickly round up the culprits and have them shot. (Or, if they were lucky, sent to Siberia for 20 or 30 years as slave labor.)

This explains, at least in part, why the people are deserting the Russian Orthodox Church in droves. There's been almost a mass exodus out of the Orthodox Church and into a bewildering variety of other sects. In the subway one finds strange, Eastern faiths and American-made proselytizers handing out their literature, alongside the vendors of pornographic magazines. The Moonies are here, as is the Church of Scientology and Hare Krishna. All three are competing with the Mother-of-God church, the White Brotherhood ("the world will end on November 24, 1993" — so you will not get the opportunity to read this book), and Vissarion, who is the reincarnation of Christ.

The Orthodox Church, acting reflexively in its old role as a state-protected institution, has called for the banning of these new upstarts and strange sects. But that will have to wait for a few more turns of the wheel back to good old-fashioned Russian despotism.

Eighty percent of the churches in Russia were destroyed by Lenin's Bolsheviks. The only reason these atheistic fanatics didn't destroy the other 20 percent was because the structures were convenient for storage of cement and the like, and a few were used as workers' museums.

The most tragic of these attacks on the symbols and dwellings of Christianity was the destruction of the Church of Christ the Savior in Moscow. At 250 feet high, it was the largest church in Russia, covering an entire city block.

God had been declared dead and so in 1936 this great symbol of Russian Christianity was attacked with an unbelievable ferocity. Its magnificent architecture was an offense to the sensibilities of good communist atheists. The building was going to be replaced by a monstrous, and typically ugly, "Palace of Soviets," topped by a gigantic statue of Godfather Lenin rising 450 feet into the sky. It was essential, you see, that Lenin reach further into the heavens than the church.

Ah, but while man proposes, God disposes. The church was so soundly built that the first dynamiting didn't bring it down. It took repeated explosions of tremendous force to make the church fall. The outbreak of World War II prevented the construction of the architectural monstrosity that was to replace Christ the Savior. So the giant hole where the church stood for 200 years was converted into the world's largest swimming pool. When I saw the pool in 1965, I noted with great pleasure that it was "temporarily in a state of repair." Instead of a gigantic statue of Lenin, it became a giant mud hole. How appropriate.

There is now "freedom of religion" in Russia, but what does that mean if the church can't get its property back? A beautiful old church in downtown St. Petersburg was also converted into a swimming pool. (The commies must have liked swimming in former churches.) Although communism is supposedly dead, the church can't get its property back. The nomenklatur, which is still very much alive, wants to keep the swimming pool and to hell with the church. Thus far, they have had their way.

St. Isaac's Cathedral, one of the most beautiful churches in the world, was turned into a museum by the communists. The church, the people, and the Ministry of Culture all want to return the cathedral to the Russian Orthodox Church, from whom the magnificent structure was confiscated in 1918. The "museum directors," all of them unreconstructed communist bureaucrats, refuse to give up the property (from which they are undoubtedly stealing money from the admissions price). They say they will close the building "for repairs" if any move is made by the church to retrieve the property.

The birth of the buttocks

You can't talk about religion in Russia without discussing Darwinism and Lemarkism, the heart and soul of the theology of communism.

Stalin was a true believer in the theories of Lemark and Darwin (everybody believes in *something*). Any scientist who did not so believe was "dismissed" (shot). As there was no god (so you had to spell it in the lower case), then Darwin and Lemark had to be right.

Lemarkian theory goes something like this: If you cut the tails off enough puppies for enough generations, then they will eventually be born with no tails. The tail will become stumpy and pass into the category of a "vestigial organ," that is, a vestige of its former friendly, wagging self.

Now, Darwin was more into the positive end of things and therein lies the story of the Birth of the Buttocks. The round, sometimes attractive area that you sit on is quite utilitarian and man has always been fascinated with it (especially on a woman). The reason that the Great Developer put a buttocks on humans is because one can't just sit on bones, in this case your ischial tuberosities, covered with nothing but a thin layer of skin.

The "natural selection" wizards apparently believe that those unfortunate early humans who were non-calipigenous (sans buttocks) developed pressure sores and, as there were no antibiotics, electrical massaging beds, or debriding surgeons to attend them, they all died of septicemia, probably from E. coli bacteria, which were here long before we were (or so they say).

But those lucky near-humans who had a little fat on their buttocks-to-be did not develop pressure sores and thus were "selected" to survive and give man something to sit on. The fat was obviously placed there by the Great Evolver for the very purpose of making man calipigenous. It was also a great boon to the garment industry and, incidentally, some non-garment industries, such as pornography and Rubens-type paintings.

Evolution was an integral part of the Marxist philosophy's "scientific proof" that man can be reformed by man and thus made perfect: transformed into the new Soviet man who will worship and serve the state, which is merely an extension of himself.

So this childish Darwinian and Lemarkian thinking dominated Russian science, at least on the surface, for 75 years. Of course, few really believed it outside of Stalin's immediate circle of psychotic sycophants.

Oddly enough, it was the *West* that embraced Darwin's theories with both arms, in spite of their humanist, anti-Christian content and lack of any evidence that one type of animal evolved from another. Strange, isn't it?

Bewitched and bewildered

On to more pleasant things — such as my first date with Leda.

We had agreed to meet at Dom Kinige on Nevsky Prospekt on Sunday afternoon at 4:00. I arrived early (of course) and settled down to wait. But Leda appeared just a few moments later. She was part of a great crowd of people emptying out of the subway across the street. The large collar of her coat and a purple shawl framed a face no cosmetic could improve: a little lipstick, nothing more. If anything, she looked even more beautiful in full light.

We walked the avenues and byways of the city for two hours. I tried to pay attention to her commentary on the points of interest, but it was difficult. None of it could compare with the feminine, magical creature with her arm entwined with mine.

"Beel, this is the former palace of Count Beloselsky-Belozersky. Do you like it?"

"Hmm, yes, quite nice." Even with our heavy coats on, I could feel her breast against my arm.

"Dom Kinige was supposed to be ten stories high, but the Czar ruled that no building could be higher than the Admiralty. It was quite a good decision, don't you think?"

"What? Oh, yes, quite wise."

"Beel, is there something wrong?" I couldn't hold it back any longer: "No, my precious, voluptuous beauty. Everything is quite perfect."

I had spoken rapidly and she didn't understand every word. But my expression and tone of voice apparently conveyed my meaning. She moved us onto safer ground. "So, Beel, what do Americans think of the new Russia?"

I took up the new theme with feigned enthusiasm and expostulated on the vagaries of politics. The time passed too quickly; we had to part. I had to fix a time for meeting her again. I had planned it well in advance.

"Leda, there's a Christmas dinner with ballet at the Grand Hotel Europe on Christmas eve. I would be most honored if you would come with me."

"Oh, no, Beel, I'm going to Latvia with friends for the New Year; I couldn't."

Going to Latvia with "*friends?*" What did THAT mean? But why was I getting so upset? I'd just met this woman. What difference did it make?

I fought off panic. Perhaps she didn't understand that I wasn't talking about New Year's Eve, the big event of the year here, but merely Christmas, which in Russia is just another day at the office.

I decided that there just HAD to be a communications problem. I guided our stroll toward the Hotel Europe. The girl at the desk could explain what I meant.

"Well, here we are at the Europe," I said casually. "Why don't we have a cup of coffee?" She thought that would be nice. We had the coffee and then I suggested we visit the front desk to clarify this business of the dinner party. (It occurred to me, somewhere along here, that maybe she thought I was asking her to spend the night with me at the hotel. Language misunderstandings can be hilarious or tragic; I've made both.)

The girl grasped the problem at once. There was a long interchange between them in Russian, not a word of which I understood. But at the end, Leda turned to me and said, "horoshow." THAT I understood — everything was okay.

Our dinner party on Christmas eve was a great success. We saw a ballet from Swan Lake, performed by the St. Petersburg Ballet Company. Before that, a 12-piece string orchestra played Strauss waltzes during our dinner of pheasant and champagne.

I learned over dinner that my beautiful Leda had never experienced such an evening. This brilliant girl, with a degree in engineering *and* music, had never before enjoyed the very music she had studied in such opulent surroundings. It was like knowing a language fluently, but never visiting the country where it was spoken. She had been to the theatre, of course, but she had never been inside the marble halls of the Grand Hotel Europe or seen a performance here.

It was a magical St. Petersburg evening for both of us — one I'm sure neither of us will ever forget. We made plans for another date as soon as she returned from her trip to Latvia with "friends."

Later on that evening, my paranoia kicked into overdrive. It's almost *too* perfect, I said to myself. Why would a gorgeous 31-year-old woman be interested in a man decidedly on the down-side of the longevity curve? I could think of only four possible explanations.

1. I am devastatingly handsome with a matching personality.

2. I am rich by Russian standards.

3. She is a KGB agent.
4. She is a prostitute.

It couldn't be 4; that would have been revealed by now. Number 1 is not a tenable hypothesis either, as my editor, my mother, and any honest acquaintance will attest. (Don't be fooled by the photograph on my newsletter — it's my high-school graduation picture.)

Number 2 is undoubtedly true, but I didn't have the impression that it meant very much to Leda. Hmmmm, that left number 3.

I remembered the story of Tyler Kent. You'd have to be an extremely well-read anti-communist to have heard of him. He was on the staff of the U.S. embassy in Russia just before the start of World War II. He fell in love with a Russian girl who admitted she was in the employ of the KGB. They just learned to live with it — and for a while, they had a marvelous time together.

Later, Kent was sentenced to a long prison term in a secret trial in England, not because he betrayed any secrets to Russia, but because he knew too much about FDR's secret maneuverings to get us into World War II. Kent died recently in Tyler, Texas, without, as far as I know, ever telling his side of the story. I wonder how they kept him silent all those years?

What does all this have to do with my beautiful Leda? Probably nothing. I don't know any state secrets and, besides, she wouldn't turn me in even if I did — would she?

I decided that if she is in the employ of the KGB, I'll just ask her to level with me and everything will be fine. Maybe I'll *pretend* to be guarding some important secrets, just to keep her interested in me.

Besides, I could use a little more excitement in my life.

A quick postscript: Craig is back in St. Petersburg. From the fire back to the frying pan, so to speak. He's got a great job with an American bank here. But he says he would have come back anyway; he'd missed his raven-haired girlfriend too much. He told me, "Some things are worth dying for." With Leda and all, I guess it's just as well he didn't give me her number.

Chapter Eighteen
The Fast Train to Vologda

In late February, in two feet of snow, I took the "fast train" to Vologda. It is one of Russia's legendary hamlets, filled with 18th and 19th century wooden homes and churches. Vologda is about 450 miles east of St. Petersburg; you reach it on a special express called the White Nights. This ground-hugging comet streaked through the snow-covered birch and fur forests at an average speed of 30 miles an hour. Even that seemed too fast to me.

The lurching, swaying trains of Russia are death traps. The rail beds are over a hundred years old and have been poorly maintained. The washboard roadbed and the weaving of the tracks make the ride more like being on a bumpy highway than on a train. The coaches constantly bang against each other with a terrible crash. You wonder which will come first — will the coupling fail and the cars fly apart, leaving the passengers stranded in the freezing cold Russian night? Or will the next car finally bash this one to pieces?

Derailments are quite common and collisions are regular items in the "incidence" reports. The mortality and morbidity figures sound like a report from a war zone. In 1992 alone, there were 371 fatalities as a result of 508 "incidents." And these are only the figures for the October Railroad in Russia's northwest.

Until recently, these annual figures were a carefully guarded state secret. No one realized that the Soviet rail system was actually more dangerous than Aeroflot, which is recognized by at least one international travel organization as the world's worst airline.

A third possibility occurred to me: We could be attacked by bandits, stripped of all our possessions, and tossed into the snow. Those are the sort of thoughts that assail you on a long, cold train ride across Russia. I took another swig of Rossiyskaya vodka (just for medicinal purposes, you understand) and tried to nap.

There are a number of diseases one can contract from riding the rails in Russia, such as fungus infections, scabies, bed lice, and maybe even a little touch of tuberculosis. The reason for this menu of undesirables is that the managers of each coach, women who make about $5 a month, pocket the money that should be spent at the laundry and just re-press the linen after each use. When you ride the rails in Russia, bring your own bedding — at the very least your own pillow case. You'll be glad you did.

Not quite the Ritz

The lobby of the hotel in Vologda had the usual early 20th century ambience. You'd recognize it as bus station decor. Eight people were patiently waiting at the check-in counter, while the two female clerks carried on an animated conversation about last night's party and how Olga made a fool of herself.

In due Soviet time, we were attended to and I was offered a regular room with a broken toilet seat for $3 a night (special high price for rich American tourist), or a *suite* with a broken toilet seat for 50 cents more. I decided to splurge and ordered the suite. But no, the clerk decided, there were no suites available; there was a rock band in town and they had taken all the suites, regardless of the condition of their toilet seats.

The clerk looked at me with the typical deadpan face of a bureaucrat. (Why do I have to miss the TV soap opera to deal with you? Why are you even on this earth?) She seemed to be waiting for me to make the difficult decision between having a regular room or no room. I opted for the former.

The clerks lacerated poor Olga a bit more, then finally (and reluctantly) gave me a key and condescended to wait on the next exhausted customer. Like me, he had been up all night on the White Nights express.

But it turned out my non-suite was really okay. Unlike my room in Novgorod, I could open the bathroom door without having to open the door to the hall, a real plus. On the basis of this, I'll give the hotel a rating of two garlic buds.

There is a beautiful monastery in Vologda that almost made riding the White Nights worth the risk. It was a donation from the family of Ivan the Terrible. They felt guilty, I guess, because of Ivan's bad habit of seizing everyone's wealth and killing them.

Ivan became a monk near the end of his life. He was trying to sneak into heaven with a late good showing of piety and contriteness, I suspect. He had a 20th century counterpart in Uganda's notorious butcher, Idi Amin. I trust that both have descended to their eternal reward.

Holy water and angels' tears

Let me tell you about the Rossiyskaya vodka, mentioned above, which I credit with saving my life (or at least my sanity) during my year in Russia. The label states that it is an "ecologically pure product" of 100% grain-neutral spirits. That means it's industrial grade alcohol cut with water to 80 proof. This product, if you can believe it, is better than combined holy water, angels' tears, and the sweat of Buddha. Here's what the label says:

> This genuine Russian vodka is produced according to a unique process by the Russiyskaya Korona firm which is unrivaled throughout the world for making ecologically pure products. The drink has an important curatives effect which was confirmed by medico-biological research and an international commission of experts.
>
> Moderate and prescribed use of the drink diluted with ice to 30 percent proof provides a prophylactic and curative effect for radioactive, oncological, and gastroenterological

diseases, and stabilizes psychophysical and cardiovascular systems, as well as metabolic and immunological processes.

The label was printed before the AIDS crisis developed, and clearly an upgrade is needed. Curing AIDS should be "nea problema" for Russiyskaya Korona.

Easter at the Museum of Atheism

It's ten days after Easter for the rest of the world. But here in Russia, Easter is this weekend. Do they do *everything* differently here?

I thought it would be interesting to visit the magnificent Kazan Cathedral for the Russian Orthodox Easter service, a rite that had been prohibited in Russia for 75 years. I wanted to experience the surge of emotion and the thrill of freedom these people would feel as the priest started his appeal to God for the blessing of all those present in this former cathedral that for seven decades had been a museum of atheism.

Being the emotional sort, and feeling very strongly about freedom, I knew that I would have a hard time holding back my tears.

When we arrived at the cathedral, I found I needn't have brought my handkerchief. There was a sign scrawled on the door: "*The museum is closed for the Easter holidays.*" The tears would have to wait another day.

The church *did* find a home for their Easter service, I'm happy to report. They were permitted to rent their own St. Issac's Cathedral from the state for a few hours Sunday afternoon.

At least this year, they were granted permission to hold a service. For the past 75 years, the answer had been "nyet."

Chapter Nineteen

A Litany of
Death and Disasters

On March 24, 1992, there was an explosion at the Leningrad Atomic Energy Station (LAES) and Reactor Number Three was shut down. This plant is 30 miles west, and upwind, from my apartment. (I wish they had placed the plant to the *east*, and thus downwind, from Russia's second largest city.)

As it happens, I had left for the United States that very morning. The explosion was reported on St. Petersburg radio at 9:00 am. Two hours later, the plant's press center was denying that anything untoward had happened.

Remembering the attempted cover-up at Chernobyl, and knowing this reactor was of identical design, the denial caused many of my fellow residents of St. Petersburg to panic. I don't blame them. Had I been there, I would have been on the next train to Helsinki. Heck, I might have even taken Aeroflot!

When I returned to St. Petersburg, the trees and shrubs were not aglow, the sky was not green, and the people weren't bleeding from the nose. The genie was apparently successfully put back into the bottle.

You may have read about this close call in your local paper on March 25, as I did in Atlanta. But you didn't read about the meltdown of a reactor core in the Ural Mountains on November 30, 1975. The amount of radioactive particles released then was twice that of the Hiroshima explosion. Some 450,000 people from 13 regions and two major cities were contaminated.

These people were resoaked with radiation in two other major disasters which were never reported to the outside world or to the hapless victims. They only found out what had been done to them when they started dying from cancer and thrombocytopenia.

In a five-year period, 2.7 million curies of radioactive waste were dumped into the Techa River, thus poisoning five OTHER rivers and injuring or killing more untold tens of thousands of people.

Ten years later, in 1985, there was another disaster at the Mayak Nuclear Weapons Facility, site of the above-mentioned holocaust. This time, 60,000 people were contaminated. The weapons factory that has produced this radioactive hell stores a billion curies worth of accumulated radioactive waste. That is the equivalent of 20 Chernobyls. We will probably never know how much death and human suffering has been caused by this one facility.

There are no plans for closing the Mayak plant. But the government has promised that it will "improve health care" in the region and "provide them (the residents) with a normal life."

Two questions come to mind:

1. How can you "provide them a normal life" when you are continuing to shower them with radioactive waste?

2. How do you provide "a normal life" for tens of thousands of dead and dying people?

A threat to Norway as well

Another disaster-in-the-making is developing in the northern city of Murmansk. Many of the victims of the coming tragedy will be Norwegians, in addition to numerous Russians.

Unless you are a geography buff, you may not be aware that Russia and Norway share a common border. Norway wraps around the top of Sweden and Finland to join with Russia. The port of Murmansk is only 23 miles from that border. As you can appreciate, what happens in that area is of great concern to the Norwegian government — and there is PLENTY happening.

The Russian nuclear submarine fleet at the Murmansk base is breaking up, as are the storage facilities housing 12,000 spent rods and tons of radioactive waste. Many of these spent fuel rods lie in a few meters of water less than a mile from Murmansk and its 500,000 inhabitants. Fifty abandoned submarines, containing hot reactors and rods, lie "mothballed" in the harbor. The abandoned storage ship *Lepse* is now contaminated with at least one million curies of radiation.

Workers found that some of the rods on the *Lepse* expanded, probably due to improper storage in the salty, damp environment, and they wouldn't fit into their storage containers. So they attempted to hammer the rods in with sledge hammers! Many of them broke, creating another serious risk. As the ship is a serious radiation hazard, it has been fenced off from the rest of the rusting fleet — with string.

One Russian organization which monitors such things says there have been at least 28 unreported accidents in the nuclear submarines of the North Fleet. Where the subs are, and how much radioactive material they are leaking, no one in authority will say — and perhaps don't know.

Protect us from the protectors

During one of my trips to the Big Potato, I decided to visit the Kurchatov Institute, Russia's most prestigious nuclear research center. I should not have been surprised by what I saw, but in truth, I was appalled.

A visit to the facility is more like visiting a junk yard than a research institution. Rusty cranes, looking like giant, frozen praying mantis, hover over long-abandoned construction sites. Discarded rusty pipes, metal containers, cans, paper, a broken thermos bottle, an old boot, and other trash litters the streets between institute buildings. When I was there, a group of workers were squatting in a semicircle, roasting pigs' feet with a welder's torch. Yum.

According to test results, the level of competence at the facility is appallingly low. Three of the "experts" responsible for safety of the nuclear reactors at the institute failed an exam on elementary nuclear safety measures. The 50-year-old reactors are as little as 150 yards away from the living quarters of many of the institute's employees. Reflecting the lack of confidence in their own prestigious institute, one can see a geiger counter on every apartment balcony. Everyone wants to be the first to flee when they start ticking like mad.

Vladimir Kuznetsov, head of Boris Yeltsin's radiation safety committee, was quoted as saying, "Not one nuclear power station in Russia is safe." Russian officialdom took immediate action: They forced Kuznetsov to quit his job. If he's smart, he'll take advantage of the opportunity and move his family to the Black Sea, thus avoiding thrombocytopenia, nose bleeds, and a hemorrhagic death.

Some have suggested closing down all of Russia's nuclear power plants. Just shutting the ones in the St. Petersburg district would leave 45 percent of the city in the dark and the cold. Going back to fossil-fuel plants would require 14,000 tons of coal per day to supply enough energy to keep this one city functioning. The coal industry is in a shambles and couldn't provide the coal anyway.

The answer to this extremely serious problem is not to abandon nuclear energy; it is to use it safely. Everybody sophisticated in the energy field, including even some of the greenies, knows that atomic power is here to stay. We're simply not going to go back to the 19th century, with its smoke-spewing plants and all the human suffering they caused.

Besides, the Russian bureaucracy can turn *any* project into an unmitigated disaster. Consider the following.

Some hydroelectric disasters

Russian engineers, under the orders of their unqualified superiors in the Kremlin, managed to obliterate the entire Aral Sea, one of the world's great lakes, with a bountiful supply of fish and a beautiful lakeshore. This was done to irrigate arid land to the southeast. Now the lake, seventh largest in the world, is gone; the fishing and tourist industries have been destroyed; and the land below it is as arid as ever.

Oh, the wonders of socialist planning!

The Caspian Sea, an even more important waterway for the survival of Russia, barely escaped the same fate. Someone noticed that the lake had been receding for several years, so Soviet engineers were ordered to find out why and to solve the problem.

Experts on the ecology of this, the largest lake in the world in surface area, pointed out that historically the lake receded about every 100 years. If the engineers would just leave it alone, they said, it would eventually refill. But Soviet planners were not about to be talked out of a billion-ruble five-year plan. They ordered a dam built on the lake's natural outlet to the east, called Monster Mouth.

Soon after the dam was completed, the lake decided to refill itself. The dam cannot let the water out fast enough. Now, the lake is eight feet above flood level and continues to rise. This has resulted in the flooding of millions of acres of valuable farmland around the lake. Losses are estimated in the *hundreds* of billions of rubles.

The important port of Baku has been ruined. All of the docks are under water and will soon be washed away, because the engineers who built them heeded the advice of Moscow's experts — who said the water level was going to fall.

Finally, a new group of "experts" admitted that a mistake had been made. The dams that blocked the natural drainage of the lake have been blown up. But it will take generations for the land to recover, if it ever does. Baku is simply out of business. The Russians not only lost an important port, they also lost one of their most important sources of hard currency, since shippers of oil, caviar, and other goods paid *dollars* to use the port's facilities. Symbolic of this communist-created disaster are the 16,000 tons of Azerbaijani cotton which were left, rotting and water-soaked, on the docks.

No area of the country has been spared the ecological disasters meted out by socialist planners. In Siberia, the dam for the Krasnarask hydroelectric power plant is immense — almost three kilometers across. When its builders blocked the river and flooded thousands of acres of forest, they didn't bother to cut the trees down. Ten years later, the now dead trees came free from the lake bottom and jammed the drainage of the dam. Now the Krasnarask power plant can't produce a single volt of electricity.

The Ingmurigess Station dam on the Ingure River in Georgia was an even greater fiasco. Unlike the Krasnarask structure, this dam is very narrow, but extremely high. In order to take advantage of the high water pressure, and thus generate more power at less cost, the engineers decided to place the outlets for the turbines almost at the bottom of the dam.

But in typical bureaucratic fashion, they failed to consider the consequences of their plan. Fifty kilometers away, where the Ingure empties into the Black Sea, there was a beautiful beach resort. The beach was constantly being eroded by the currents in the lake. But the Ingure has a very sandy bottom and the erosion was always counterbalanced by the sand deposits from the river. It was one of nature's fine balancing acts.

When the river was blocked by the dam, the sand quickly built up and plugged the turbines, thus rendering the power plant useless. Unfortunately, it also utterly destroyed the lake's beach, because sand from the river was no longer being deposited on it, to replace the erosion by the lake currents. The lakefront condominiums are now condemned and abandoned, as erosion eats away at their foundations. They will soon be IN the lake rather than beside it — new monuments to the wisdom of socialist planning.

Tunnels, trains, ships, and more

One of the greatest man-made disasters of all time took place at the Salang Pass between Russia and Afghanistan. The sloping Salang Pass tunnel is designed for one-way traffic only. A tanker full of gasoline collided head-on with a Soviet military convoy and burst into flames. Scores of vehicles quickly became jammed into the tunnel from both entrances. Vehicles were kept running because of the extreme cold. Both ends of the tunnel were blocked off by the military — they thought it was some kind of guerilla raid. The troops and civilians began to choke on the engine fumes. Flaming gasoline poured down the slope, setting more trucks on fire.

The tunnel became a sealed inferno. There was no escape. Panic broke out and the troops began firing at one another. Imagine, if you can, over 2,000 screaming people roasting to death in a vast underground oven.

In the Byelo-Russian city of Minsk, a large factory for electronic equipment was built and opened with the usual socialist fanfare. Soon after opening, the concrete second floor collapsed and crushed 200 workers to death.

In Georgia, after one of the worst earthquakes in recorded history, all the buildings in the capital collapsed, *except* for the ones built before the Great October Socialist Revolution.

The cruise ship *Admiral Nakhimov*, one of the Soviet Union's largest, set sail at midnight from the Black Sea port of Novorossiysk on an overnight cruise to Batumi, near the Turkish border. The sea was glassy calm and visibility was unlimited — lights could be seen 20 miles away.

An hour out of port, the captain was drunk and asleep in his cabin. A freighter approached from the southeast on a collision course. Although they had ample time to take corrective action, probably 20 minutes or more, and each was clearly visible to the other, each vessel held to its course and they crashed head on. Huge gaping holes in both ships quickly sucked in the sea and they went, sterns up, to the bottom. Over 500 souls are entombed in the wreckage.

But for total ineptitude, it is hard to top the case of the *Musson*, an anti-missile cruiser in the Russian fleet. The *Musson* was engaged with others in anti-missile defense exercises in the Pacific when a dummy cruise missile was fired at it.

Although the *Musson* fired everything it had at the incoming missile, including two anti-missile rockets and a cloud of artillery fire, the cruise missile struck the nerve center of the ship. Although the missile was not armed, the remaining fuel in the rocket spilled over the boat, caught fire, and quickly burned through the highly flammable aluminum-magnesium hull and into the ammunition storage compartments. Twenty missiles and 1,000 artillery shells exploded and the ship went quickly to the bottom with half its crew.

It proves you don't have to have missiles with warheads to sink a Russian ship — a dummy will do. As almost all Russian war ships are made of the same magnesium alloy, they are potential flaming coffins waiting to go off.

There was a lot of fanfare in the press last year about Russia releasing information about accidents that had, previously, been suppressed. But the *Musson* fiasco only made the press because of a leak at naval headquarters. When asked to explain why this accident was not reported, the official reply was: "This was not an 'accident,' it was a catastrophe — and we don't report catastrophes." How many of THOSE have they had?

All these stories of Soviet screw-ups might be funny if it weren't for the human tragedy of innocent people being crushed to death under great slabs of concrete; burned alive in tunnels; drowned in exploding submarines and ship collisions; killed in nuclear accidents (some worse than Chernobyl); buried alive in mines; smashed in thousands of traffic accidents due to drunk drivers and drunk pedestrians; and dismembered in train collisions and derailments.

The toll caused by Russia's incompetent rulers is enough to fill you with awe. It is virtually awful. And I'm afraid it will get worse.

Put the blame at the top

With all the brilliant scientists and engineers that Russia undoubtedly possesses, why the endless string of disasters and catastrophes? Why can't they get it right?

The answer is that the country has been led by ignorant peasants for more than 70 years, and it still is today. You will almost never find a political leader who has a college education or speaks a second language. Most of them don't have the talent to run a shoe-repair shop, much less a nation of 300 million people.

Mikhail Gorbachev perfectly epitomizes this ignorance and incompetence. This peasant from southern Russia so enamored the American press that many silly American liberals said they wished he could run for President of the United States! One American commentator was so carried away with Mikey that he said he qualified "for a bust on Mount Rushmore."

This vainglorious hack once decreed that the street vendors in Russia could no longer sell the traditional nesting dolls with his face on them. (Open the largest and you will find a Lenin inside a Stalin, inside a Khrushchev, inside a Brezhnev, etc.) This extremely stupid man is supposed to have a college education, but it's hard to believe, as he doesn't even have a good command of the Russian language.

Stalin's Russian was even worse, but at least he had an excuse — he wasn't Russian, but Georgian. (Stalin used to trail off the ends of his sentences because he was unsure of the proper declension.)

Gorbachev allegedly wanted to do something about the Soviet Union's alcoholism problem. So he had all the grape vines in the U.S.S.R. torched, or at least all he could find. But Russian alcoholics don't drink wine; they drink cologne, rubbing alcohol, pure ethyl, 200-proof medicinal alcohol, and vodka made from barley, wheat, or anything else that is biodegradable. So Gorby wiped out the wine and grape industry in his homeland, while alcoholism is as big a problem as ever.

This paragon of peristroika also earned the undying enmity of the Russian people for attempting to destroy one of their few pleasures: getting so blind drunk you'll forget where you are (here) and where you're going (nowhere).

There's one other communist "leader" you need to know a little bit about. The gloomy tyrant, Leonid Brezhnev, followed Khrushchev and seemed to rule forever — 17 years. He was such a miser that he made his wife save old batteries. He said "they might be useful someday." To prove that he was a great leader, Brezhnev would award himself medals several times a year. He always wanted to be the Hero of This and Hero of That.

It is not recorded what Mrs. Brezhnev did with all those spent batteries, collected over a lifetime, after Brezhnev passed on to that subterranean Hall of Communist Heroes. Maybe she decided they were useful after all and dumped them in his casket, as ballast to keep him where he belongs.

Chapter Twenty
Russia's Remarkable History

I'll make you a deal:

I won't promise any incredible sex in this chapter if you'll read it anyway.

It contains a lot of history you really should know. And you'll meet two of the most remarkable women Russia produced in this century — Fanny Kaplan, the accused near-assassin of Lenin, and Olga Damidoff, one of the most remarkable freedom fighters in history.

And you'll also learn how close the world came to being spared the terrible scourge of Soviet communism.

By July 4, 1917, it appeared that the Bolsheviks were finished. The press had revealed that Lenin was a German agent; details of his financing by the Germans, including reproduction of the most incriminating documents, made front-page news in Moscow.

The Mensheviks and left-liberals were in a state of euphoria. The revelations appeared to have destroyed totally their hated and feared rivals, the Bolsheviks. In municipal elections seven weeks before the coup, the communists won only three percent of the vote. What harm could come from such an impotent party?

And yet, in four months, Russia would suffer a coup d'état and a grotesquery beyond belief. These intellectual dreamers would face their own executions in a matter of months.

All the empty-headedness, the blindness, the complete unwillingness to act in a forceful manner against a ruthless enemy was represented in Russia's last prime minister, the egotistical and unintelligent Aleksandr Fyodorovich Kerensky. Army Intelligence, members of his cabinet, the Chief of Police, and Vice Prime Minister Konovalov all warned Kerensky that a military takeover was imminent.

The army and the navy were being openly ordered not to obey the government. The top commanders would only heed directions from the military-revolutionary committee. The communists had taken over the arsenal and declared open civil war. While Kerensky was giving his final speech before the congress, a note was handed to him which announced that the revolution was underway. Instead of calling for immediate action against the communists to have them arrested, HE CONTINUED HIS SPEECH FOR ANOTHER 20 MINUTES!

Later that evening, the mentally paralyzed Karensky had yet another opportunity to save his country from the Bolsheviks. At 1:30 am on October 25, Kerensky received the representatives of the Cossack regiments, a loyal and substantial force that could have crushed the Bolsheviks easily at that time. Although they despised Kerensky because of his duplicity and incompetence, the Cossacks offered to smash the Bolsheviks if Kerensky would order the obvious: the arrest of Lenin, Trotsky, and the rest of the revolutionaries attempting to destroy the government.

Once again, Kerensky refused to act. The Cossacks retired to their barracks to await the inevitable. The enemy occupied the central telephone station and the state bank. It was all over, except for occupying the Winter Palace, which was essentially undefended. Kerensky high-tailed it to Gotchina, 40 miles to the south, ostensibly to gather troops for a counter-offensive against the communists. The offensive never came.

Kerensky subsequently escaped to the West, leaving his wife and two sons to face a life of ridicule, persecution, and possible execution by the revolutionary regime his inaction made possible.

What are we to make of Kerensky? Was he, as some have suggested, really an agent of the German high command? There is no proof that this is the case. But he could not have been more effective in the victory of communism over the democratic forces of his country.

In the summer of 1919, Kerensky represented the deposed democratic government of Russia at a peace conference in Paris. And despite the events of the previous two years, observers noted with astonishment that he had not changed — he was as dynamic, egotistical, and politically childish as ever.

One friendly biographer said that Kerensky was the naive child of St. Petersburg's white nights, which seem to have a dreamlike effect on Russian intellectuals, leaving them permanently detached from the political realities of life. That is as kind an explanation as you're likely to find anywhere.

Kerensky was the *wrong* man at the right place and the right time at a pivotal point in history. Had the *right* man occupied his position, the democrats and the army could have destroyed the Bolsheviks *even as late as 24 hours before the final assault on the Constituent Assembly.*

Isn't it interesting how often history turns on such seemingly minor events? Next, let me tell you how a pistol that *wasn't* fired affected Russia's history — and helped create a heroine you may never forget.

An aborted assassination

Almost all assassination attempts on prominent political figures end in mystery, even though most of them happen in public places and are witnessed by hundreds, or even thousands, of people. The Lincoln and Kennedy assassinations are prime examples of how these momentous events, with the ostensible capture of the assailants quickly accomplished, evolve into dark mysteries.

The "lone assassin" explanation for political killings did not originate with the shooting of President Kennedy. The terrorist plotters of the assassination attempt we are about to relate asked for official approval of the Central Committee of the Communist

Party of Russia to kill Lenin. (They said he was moving *too fast*; they were afraid his zeal could lead to their defeat.)

Although denied official blessing, they were told the committee HAD NO OBJECTION TO THE KILLING AS LONG AS IT WAS DONE AS AN "INDIVIDUAL ACT."

The following incredible story was reported by one of the participants, Boris Sokoloff, a Russian doctor who later became prominent in the West as a cancer researcher at the Pasteur Institute, Columbia University, Washington University Medical School, and Florida Southern College.

On a freezing night in October 1917, Dr. Sokoloff went with the would-be assassin, a nice man named Demidoff, who had never killed a living creature, to Lenin's secret meeting place. Remarkably, Lenin was so sure of the safety of his retreat that he dismissed his chauffeur and instructed him to come back for him at midnight.

Demidoff ascended to the third-floor apartment while Sokoloff waited in the car. He opened the door so quietly Lenin did not even turn around. Lenin was sitting in an armchair, drinking tea and talking with the building owner, Nikolai Kokko.

The back of Lenin's head was an easy target for Demidoff, just 15 feet away. He couldn't possibly miss. He raised the automatic pistol and took careful aim. In a moment, the gratitude of untold generations of Russians and the rest of mankind would be his.

But Demidoff couldn't pull the trigger. He froze in place for several moments, then slinked back down the stairs. In the car he whined to Sokoloff, "I couldn't overcome my feelings and shoot him. It was justified murder, I know. But all my upbringing revolted against it."

Three months after the fall of the democratic government, Demidoff made a second attempt on Lenin's life, this time with bullets and dynamite. He was more determined than ever because, two months earlier, Lenin had done exactly what he said he was going to do: He had taken over the government with a small band of killers and bank robbers.

On the night of January 1, 1918, Demidoff and his two accomplices, Spiridinov, a courageous soldier and anti-communist, and Safronov, a steel worker who also hated the Bolsheviks, waited at the bridge across the Moika River where they knew Lenin would pass in his car as he returned from a rally.

Again, the gods of the darker recesses acted against the hapless Demidoff. Spiridinov was stationed under the bridge and was told to detonate the bomb when the limousine was halfway across. The car approached slowly in the thick snow and inched its way across the bridge. When it was halfway over, Demidoff gave the signal. But nothing happened.

Demidoff was only ten feet away and saw Lenin clearly. He grabbed his pistol and opened fire on the car. He was sure he had killed Lenin, but in fact the communist mastermind was not even wounded.

Sitting in the back seat with Lenin was Fritz Platten, the very man who had acted as conduit for funds to Lenin from the German high command. Platten saw the gun and quickly pushed Lenin to the floor. The car raced off into the darkness; the only injury was a bullet graze to Platten's finger.

When he crawled from under the bridge, Spiridinov apologized sheepishly: "I lost my nerve. There was an innocent man in Lenin's car." Demidoff flew into a rage and threw the bomb into the Moika River, where it exploded harmlessly.

The story of Fanny Kaplan

Eight months later, on August 30, 1918, a Demidoff protege named Fanny Kaplan was said to have shot Lenin, almost fatally, with a Browning automatic pistol containing "poisoned bullets." As he was about to enter his car, three shots were fired, the story goes, and Lenin fell to the pavement unconscious. He had been shot in the neck, with the bullet piercing the apex of the lung. He was taken to the Kremlin at high speed, bleeding profusely and appearing near death. He could barely move and his pulse was very weak. It was assumed that he would die before dawn.

The very next day, Bukharin, writing in *Pravda*, gave the following preposterous report: "Lenin, shot through twice, with pierced lungs, spilling blood, refuses help and goes on his own. The next morning, still threatened by death, he reads papers, listens, learns, observes to see that the engine of the locomotive that carries us toward global revolution has not stopped working."

Refuses help and goes on his own? Near death and reading the papers? No wonder the doctors got no credit and no one today can tell you who treated the Great Man. Gods don't need doctors to help them.

A major wound to the neck at the angle of the jaw would almost certainly cause some serious paralysis. Lenin recovered with no evidence of neurological damage. There is not a single photograph extant of Lenin showing any scar to his neck after the alleged shooting.

Whether apocryphal or not, the assassination attempt sealed the fate of Russia. Lenin was unknown in the West before the attack and was practically unknown in Russia, outside his adoring circle of fellow revolutionaries.

Fanny Kaplan was arrested the night of the attack. Although there was no trial and no court verdict from the Council of People's Commissars or the Cheka, it was reported that she was executed "while trying to escape" a few days later. Her remains were allegedly "destroyed without a trace."

Historian Richard Pipes commented on the dramatic death of a woman accused of murder, but never tried: "Thus perished a young woman ridiculed as the Russian Charlotte Corday: without the semblance of a trial, shot in the back while the truck engines roared to drown out her screams, her corpse disposed of like so much garbage."

While certainly dramatic, the execution story is probably a fake. Numerous reports from former prisoners in the gulag, and even prison guards, reveal that Fanny Kaplan lived in relative luxury in prison and was alive 30 years after the shooting. While in prison, she had a radio and read daily newspapers — unbelievable luxuries in the Soviet penal system.

The newspaper *Komsomolskaya Pravda* acknowledged in early 1993 that, "Great doubts have emerged as to whether there was indeed an attempt on Lenin's life." Remember that the Bolsheviks often used staged-assassination attempts as an excuse for persecuting and murdering their opposition. Fanny Kaplan's alleged assassination attempt resulted in severe repressions against the opponents of the Bolsheviks.

"We call on all comrades to maintain complete calm and to intensify their work in combating counter-revolutionary elements," one 1918 statement proclaimed. And it promised: "The working class will respond to attempts against its leaders with even greater consolidation of its forces, with merciless mass terror against all enemies of the Revolution." (Note that "merciless mass terror" is how the Bolsheviks "maintain complete calm.")

The strange story of Lee Harvey Oswald

Let me interrupt my narrative of 77-year-old assassination attempts to tell you something about one that changed the course of *our* history three decades ago. I'm referring, of course, to Lee Harvey Oswald's murder of John F. Kennedy.

You haven't read about it in the American press, but many people in Minsk, Byelorussia, where Oswald was supposedly trained as a marksman, knew him well and totally disbelieve the assassination accounts. The Oswald who emerges from their memories doesn't fit the one we have been told about.

Ernst Titovets, Pavel, and Ella knew Oswald well when he lived in Russia from 1959 to 1962. In separate interviews, they all said he was a patriotic American who knew little about Marxist theory. The two men also said he was a poor shot. Yet he was supposed to have disposed of the President with three accurate shots at 100 yards and in less than six seconds — using a World War II Italian rifle!

Titovets, a research neurologist, spent many evenings talking with Oswald and is convinced he knew nothing about communist ideology. "Lee didn't know anything about communism," he said. All three friends believe that Oswald was a set up "by some elements in the U.S. government" to take the blame for the assassination. Titovets called him "an attractive cold war patsy."

Ella, a math teacher, says she thought Oswald was a CIA spy. That doesn't mean much, because every Russian was told that *every* American who travelled abroad in the '50s and '60s was "a CIA spy." Oswald proposed to her, but she turned him down as "I had no deep feelings for him."

Pavel said, "After the assassination, everybody tried to make him out as an idiot, but he was a normal guy. Oswald was never dangerous."

In an interview in Moscow in September 1992, Marina Oswald, Lee's Russian wife at the time of the assassination, contradicted her testimony before the Warren Commission. She now maintains that he was not guilty.

Reading all of this in Russia, I wondered how much would appear in the American press. Friends later told me the answer was just what I expected: nothing.

If you find all of this unbelievable, and you recoil from the idea of a U.S. government plot, read the book, *JFK — A Conspiracy of Silence*, by Dr. Charles A. Crenshaw. He was the surgeon who attended Kennedy when he was brought to Parkland Hospital, essentially dead. You will never again think of Oswald as a "lone assassin" — or even an accomplice in the murder of the century.

Some courageous women

Back to one last story about the pathetic and ineffective would-be assassin, Demidoff. (Don't judge him too harshly; he turns into a hero at the end.)

During the last stand against the Bolsheviks, Demidoff was at the Winter Palace and he was as pitiful as ever. "We are defeated," he muttered. "We deserve this. We softhearted intellectuals, we must take our punishment right up to the end.... Our destiny is to be defeated in glory, like the first Christians."

But the senior officers present didn't seek glory. They wanted to surrender "to avoid bloodshed." Then occurred one of those ironic and amazing coincidences of war. A small group of defenders arrived at the Winter Palace, including a battalion of *women*.

The girls were tall, athletic, and carried their rifles like professionals. On their shoulderboards they bore black skulls on a white background, symbolizing that they were ready to die for the cause of freedom. As they entered, Demidoff exclaimed, "My Lord! Olga brought them here!" Captain Olga Demidoff, the leader of the shock battalion, was his sister.

That evening, as the communists were closing in on the Palace, the women decided to take the battle to the enemy. They would meet the Bolsheviks in Alexander Square, on the south side of the Palace, and hold it until reinforcements sent by Kerensky arrived. (Remember my telling you, earlier in this chapter, that Kerensky fled the palace, ostensibly to gather reinforcements? Of course he never returned.)

These tough, typical Russian women charged into the semi-darkness of a deceptively beautiful and starry St. Petersburg night. They advanced across the plaza in battle formation with Olga at their head. She ordered "shoulder rifles — fire!" Demidoff, watching from a Palace window, saw that the surprise attack had gained some ground. But then, "The Bolsheviks are attacking their right flank!" he screamed.

A group of communists, hearing the gunfire, advanced from the river. As they captured a few of the battalion members, screams could be heard. The communists discovered to their amazement that the opposing forces were *women*! They tore off their victims' clothes and began raping and mutilating them.

As he witnessed the savagery, Demidoff became a man possessed. He called the palace defenders together and became their leader. "After me!" he shouted. "All of you!" With bayonets fixed, the men charged into the melee of screaming, tortured women. Their terrible ferocity drove back the enemy and Demidoff's forces managed to rescued a large portion of the women, including Olga.

They carried Olga back to the palace. A depressing pall fell over the defenders. It was clear that Kerensky's relief army was only a dream. There would be no rescue.

Dr. Sokoloff attended to Olga's wound. She was covered with mud and blood. Her only remark was a grim and determined, "We shall have revenge."

Sokoloff, Demidoff, and the women's battalion managed to escape the palace through a secret tunnel, a relic from the time of Catherine the Great. Those left in the Winter Palace when the communists stormed it were summarily executed.

There is no bronze statue to Olga Demidoff and her courageous warriors in Alexander Square — or anywhere in Russia, so far as I know. But these women are the true "Heroes of the Revolution," the accolade so often bestowed by the communists on their brigands and terrorists. I'm glad I got to know this remarkable woman. Aren't you?

Chapter Twenty-One

The West to the Rescue

Leon Trotsky was a diabolical and brilliant communist revolutionary who was so talented he became Lenin's right-hand man and the organizer of the armed bands of killers that destroyed the Russian republic. Even before the communist coup d'état in Russia, Trotsky was known worldwide as a brilliant, but vicious, international criminal whose objective was to enslave the entire world through Leninist Bolshevism.

In 1916, Trotsky was in the United States, raising funds and gathering support for the revolution. Police and immigration authorities were worried about what this dangerous man would do if he managed to return to his native Russia and join forces with Lenin. The authorities knew that Leon Trotsky was a key to the Russian revolution.

This next part will absolutely astound you. Pardon all the capital letters, but this is really important:

IT WAS THE PRESIDENT OF THE UNITED STATES, THAT FOP AND PECKSNIFF LIAR FROM PRINCETON, WOODROW WILSON, WHO PERSONALLY SAW TO IT THAT TROTSKY GOT AN AMERICAN PASSPORT AND SAFE PASSAGE THROUGH EUROPE IN ORDER TO JOIN FORCES WITH LENIN.

Trotsky, as the experts had predicted, played a key role in the overthrow of the Russian democratic republic and the consequent 70 years of darkness for all of Eastern Europe. The concatenation of events, starting with the Russian revolution, led to the horrors of the second world war and the dozens of wars since. Woodrow Wilson, who lied the American people into World War I, must bear a large portion of the blame for this Century of Slavery.

One of Wilson's biographers, Jennings C. Wise, wrote: "Historians must never forget that Woodrow Wilson, DESPITE THE EFFORTS OF THE BRITISH POLICE, made it possible for Leon Trotsky to enter Russia with an American passport." [Emphasis added.]

Wilson's behavior was so gross, and actually treasonous, that our own diplomatic corps questioned the President's actions. From the U.S. legation in Switzerland: "People are asking why the President expresses support of Bolsheviki, in view of rapine, murder, and anarchy of these bandits."

Keep in mind that at the time, we had American troops in Archangel, Russia, ostensibly for the purpose of helping the anti-communist forces in that country defeat the Bolsheviks. Our charge' d'affaires in Archangel, De Witt Poole, was so incensed that he resigned. This threw the State Department into a panic and they asked Poole to go quietly "in a natural and normal manner" in order to prevent "a grave and perhaps disastrous effect upon the morale of American troops in the Archangel district which might lead to the loss of American lives."

Stripped of its diplomatese, the State Department was saying: "We must not let the American troops (and the American people) know that the President of the United States is openly supporting our mortal enemy."

It is now clear that "right-wing" groups who said the communist revolution was nothing but a takeover by a group of ruthless criminals, financed by Germany and the United States, were absolutely correct. Few of these communist psychopaths believed the rhetoric they fed to the people and, thanks to the innate intelligence of the Russian people, only a very few uneducated peasants and airheads among the nobility supported the Bolsheviks. Sophisticated Russians knew what was happening from the beginning of the "revolution." They saw it for what it was — a coup d'état. As the editorials of the still-free press reflected in early 1918:

> If we are to believe Mr. Lenin, what is now happening in Russia is the "dictatorship of the proletariat." But if Mr. Lenin himself affirms that killing delegates, assassinations of civilians, drunken pogroms — if this is all the "dictatorship of the proletariat," then we are forced to refuse this type of government. (*Russkiye Vedomosti*, 1918)

The support from the United States came from ideological fatheads, primarily in the Ivy League colleges — czarism was "undemocratic" and had to go. It was true because Walter Duranty of the *New York Times* said so, as did many industrialists who knew what they were doing. To this day, I haven't been able to figure out why. The most likely answer is the explanation given in the book, *The Naked Capitalist*, by Cleon Skousen. You should read it, but I doubt you will find it in your library — it's too politically incorrect.

Whose side is he on?

It seems that whenever communism was about to collapse and needed support, someone in the West came to its rescue. That was true with Wilson in 1916; it was true with the Roosevelts in the 1940s (both Franklin and Eleanor were notorious for their support of communist causes and individuals); and, judging by what passes for "news" in some of our nation's press, it is still true today.

I could fill a book with examples, but I'll let just one suffice. It comes from *U.S. News and World Report*, which at one time had a well-deserved reputation for its anti-communist and pro-freedom positions.

Not any more. Under Morton Zuckerman, it has become a shocking example of how much of the press in the West tries to protect the crumbling socialist empire. Zuckerman, the owner and editor of *U.S. News and World Report*, wrote an editorial in the fall of 1992 that could have come straight out of the pages of *Pravda*.

In a venal and sarcastic attack against the forces of freedom in Russia, Zuckerman said that "Adam Smith's 'invisible hand,' which many Western economists kiss, is not liberating Russia. It is strangling it." Zuckerman bemoaned the fact that the "destruction of the communist party" (which is alive and well, but lying low) eliminated "the only bureaucracy able to carry out government decisions." Zuckerman is concerned that the communist party, one of the most terroristic organizations in human history, can't "carry out government decisions" and that "primitive capitalism of the 19th century" is the source of Russia's problems.

In 75 years, Zuckerman's beloved communists have created what may very well be an irreparable mess: the streets and roads are vintage 1930; thousands of buildings were gutted in "capital improvement" projects and have been standing empty for 20 years and will remain empty indefinitely; there's no milk, no chocolate, no lettuce, but plenty of half-rotten apples; there is trash and garbage everywhere and the subways are crumbling. Russia is a gigantic trash bin filled with dogs, cats, and people, in descending order of importance.

And Zuckerman blames this socialist hell on capitalism and "Adam Smith's invisible hand"! What in #@!& is going on here?

I don't really think that the owner and editor of *U.S. News and World Report* is a communist. I think that he is simply one of those people who sees all progress and good as emanating from government action. I'm sure he's never read *The Federalist Papers* — and wouldn't agree with them if he DID read them. Our Founding Fathers get absolutely no respect from these modern-day Jacobins, these rich, intellectual airheads, these lovers of omniscient and omnipotent government — the ones Lenin called "useful idiots."

Why are so many "liberals" in the West like this? Don't ask me, I don't know. Chalk it off to man's innate inability to appreciate the advantages of freedom and personal responsibility; blame it on a powerful and continuing conspiracy of Insiders of the CFR and Trilateral Commission; excuse it as the work of "useful idiots," as Lenin often referred to them; even call it the will of God (but if so, then God has a very strange sense of humor).

A pleasant interlude

On to a more pleasant subject. Leda and I went to the Russian Museum last night, and three hours zoomed by as Leda educated me on Russian art. She looked at the paintings, earnestly explaining the technique of the artist, his background, his other works, the duel in which he was killed.

Leda studied the paintings and I studied Leda; that was art enough for me. I'm beginning to realize that I'm well and truly smitten with this lady.

We had dinner at a very special place with soft piano and candles. Let me tell you about Leda's eyes. They're the typical Russian grey-blue, but with a special diamond-like quality when she's about to say something serious. Around her pupils is a tiny corn-yellow bracelet, like the sunflowers of the Russian steppes.

Now don't get me wrong; I'm not in love or anything. It must be the long St. Petersburg winter nights that are causing this gnawing hunger within my chest. I don't think it's a medical condition. And why do I feel like the Hunchback of Notre Dame — twisted body, bulging eyes, and writhing tongue — whenever I'm around her?

With the candles softly glowing, the piano playing "As Time Goes By," a good bottle of Georgian wine in front of us, I make my move.

"Leda, you are the most beautiful girl in Russia," I blurt out. *That* was certainly debonair! I'm met with her usual reaction: She looks down at her hands (exceptionally beautiful hands), slowly shakes her head, and makes "Beel...." a multi-syllabic word.

I do have one advantage. She wants me to improve her English and she soaks up my gentle corrections like a sponge. I don't correct ALL of her mispronunciations and grammar. I like her English just the way it is. If she becomes proficient, she may not need me any more. THAT would be a very bad thing.

I have never seen Leda's apartment. In true communist fashion, she has been forced to live in one of Khrushchev's five-story concrete dog houses with drunken Russian men and, fortunately, her brother who protects her. She is too ashamed to let me see it.

How can she come out of that squalid prison always looking stylish and radiantly beautiful? I do not know how Russian women accomplish this miracle. But I'm glad for it.

Chapter Twenty-Two

Is Communism Dead?
Don't Be Too Sure

Reading one of the English-language newspapers from Moscow, I was astounded to learn that a key participant of the Stalinist terror is still alive and well in Moscow. Although unknown to most westerners, Col. Boris Vainstein was one of the great figures of the communist empire. It is ironic that many Nazis leaders were tried, convicted, and executed under highly questionable rules of international law, but *communist* arch-criminals like this man live in comfort and respectability.

As head of "State Security Services," Vainstein was the unofficial emperor of the gulag. He was the supervisor of millions of slaves who were worked to death in Siberia during the reign of Stalin.

Vainstein spent his entire life in the dark shadows of Russia's clandestine services, from the NKVD and the Cheka to the KGB. He somehow managed to survive all the purges. He was the assassin, rather than the assassinated, and in fact was the executioner of many of his bosses.

One of the cleverest communists of them all, Vainstein is hardly ever mentioned in the histories of the Stalin era. But he was undoubtedly responsible for the deaths of hundreds of thousands, perhaps millions, of "dissidents" and slave laborers.

Now, the newspaper article revealed, he serves as a paid consultant to many Western companies and commissions as an expert in matters of industry and energy!

I decided that I *HAD* to meet this extraordinary character, so I asked Nikolai to make an appointment for me to see him at his Moscow office. It wasn't easy, but Nikolai can accomplish anything in Russia — except make money.

I arrived exactly on time. A massive thug in an ill-fitting grey suit escorted me into Vainstein's office and stood stolidly behind me, his arms folded across his chest.

It was the most frightening interview of my life. Vainstein was exactly as the newspaper article had described him — the cruel, red face, the eyes that smoked with rage, the fist almost shattering the wooden table as he thundered the litany of communist bestiality. I found him absolutely terrifying.

As I looked across the desk, I realized I was staring into the eyes of an unrepentant killer. Even in his mid-80s, Boris Vainstein was a powerful, frightening presence.

He spoke unashamedly of his prescription for Russia. "The state must be preserved. The people are merely servitors of the state," he thundered. Vainstein left no doubt that massive cruelty and suffering are the only answer.

"In order to get out of the crisis, it is essential to raise a cruel system in Russia, to introduce forced labor!" He pounded the table with his hairy fist, overturning an empty glass which began rolling toward me.

The small office was stuffy and I found it hard to breathe. My imagination began working overtime. I could almost feel the miasma of terror, the putrid smell of millions of corpses, the groans and screams of the tortured and dying.

I was afraid to move, even to intercept the rolling glass, fearful that it would be misinterpreted by the massive thing standing behind me and I'd get a bullet in my brain.

I had to get out of there ... immediately. "Well, yes, Colonel, thank you very much," I began babbling. The glass bounced off my elbow and crashed to the floor. I gave the bodyguard my most simpering, cowardly smile and moved to the door. My wet palm slid across the doorknob; the door was locked. I was close to total panic. "I'm going to die here!," I wailed to myself.

There was a buzzing sound and the door slowly swung open. I remember thinking in my temporary dementia, "I didn't know they had electronic doors in Russia."

As I reached for the door, I said something inane like, "Well, again thanks, Colonel, and have a nice day." I hurried down four flights of stairs (even a retired KGB officer doesn't merit working elevators in Russia) and burst through the front door.

I was back on the street, with its trash and litter and sweet smell of garbage — what a relief!

Boris Yeltsin and the KGB

Boris Vainstein may be near the end of his career. But what is NOT near an end is the hidden power and secret influence of Russia's most feared apparatus of the state, the KGB. It is not dead; in fact, it is not even very carefully hidden.

Boris Yeltsin knows this and, like his predecessors, he is undoubtedly part of this secret apparatus. Remember, Mikhail Gorbachev started his career as an informant for the KGB and Yeltsin was the top dog in the Ekaterinberg district — you don't get there by being a democrat or by being anti-KGB.

This alcoholic freedom-lover has been a dedicated party man all of his life — and, in spite of the brainwash of the *New York Times* and other crypto-socialist publications, there is no evidence that he has changed. Please note: *Everything Yeltsin does discourages the very freedom he claims to support!* A heavy export tax, unheard of in the free world, gives Yeltsin's government a bite out of the budding entrepreneur's capital even before he has a chance to show a profit. If he manages to make a profit, in spite of the shakedown by this "preferred partner," the businessman will then have to pay crushing taxes on these profits as well.

The West, especially the American press, is going through an adoration phase for Boris, just as it did for Mikhail. Our liberals never learn.

You need to understand that in Russia, NOTHING of substance has changed. Yet the protection and preservation of the status quo is being hailed in the West as a triumph of democracy. Did the neo-capitalistic Yeltsin overcome the resistance of the "right-wing" parliament and its major protagonist, the evil and Stalin-like Kosbulatov? Did real market reforms follow? Did the inexorable decline and collapse of Russia go into remission or even slow down? The answer to all these questions is "no."

A Colonel Cherkassov has been promoted to the rank of general. Who cares?, you ask. Cherkassov is head of the St. Petersburg branch of the Cheka/KGB/SSS/RSM and was the merciless enforcer for both Brezhnev *and* Gorbachev. If Mr. Yeltsin is such a democrat, why is he promoting this jackal to the rank of general?

I believe Yeltsin is far more dangerous than the "Stalin-like" Kosbulatov because, while Kasbulatov is obviously a maniacal, homicidal Russian bear with rabies, Western leaders *like* Yeltsin — in part, I suspect, because they have no one else in this crazy country to pin their hopes on. The same people, especially in the press, who thought Castro was the George Washington of Cuba, and Lenin was the great liberator of Russia, are chasing another dangerous dream.

Whether it's Yeltsin, Kasbulatov, or some other pretender, the KGB continues to run the show. As one Russian human-rights leader so aptly put it: "What would the world have said if, after Hitler's defeat, the Gestapo had survived and taken over? IF THE GUARDS ARE ALIVE, IT MEANS THE THINGS THEY GUARD ARE ALSO ALIVE."

The new Russian national flag is red, blue, and white. The first letter for red in Russian is a K (krasny). The first letter for blue is a G (goluboy). And the first letter for white is a B (beliy): KGB. The Russians joke about this odd coincidence in their flag colors — but it is a serious joke.

History comes full circle

When you listen to some of the political opinions of the people on the street, you have the feeling of being transported back to 1935: "I'm a Leninist and a communist. I want all nations to live in harmony."

The Russians' love of authority, ANY authority, is typified by an old man carrying a large picture of Czar Nicholas with lettering that reads, "Both Stalin and the Czar made Russia great." Now, there's a real "odd couple."

A recent visitor to Russia understood what is really happening. Stephen Handleman, a visiting scholar on Soviet studies at Columbia University, had this to say in December 1992:

> History has come full circle once again. After the events at the Congress of People's Deputies, and the spread of disillusionment with the pro-democracy forces across the old Soviet empire, fears about a revival of Stalinism — or its modern equivalents — no longer seem as absurd as they once might have.

In fact, nothing that you can imagine would be absurd in the context of contemporary Russia: there could be a swing to Jeffersonian democracy or — far more likely — a return to oriental despotism. Edward Limonov, an unrepentant degenerate and Stalin-worshiper, wrote in *Sovetskaya Rossiya* that RUSSIA MUST UNITE WITH THE ISLAMIC WORLD AGAINST THE WEST. Now isn't *that* a comforting thought?

The Nazi-like brown shirts and the communist red shirts blend together in Russia, as well they should, because the differences between them, as in 1935, are really quite trivial. Most Americans have forgotten (or never knew) that the very word "Nazi" is a contraction for "national socialism."

Both Lenin and Hitler believed in ruthless central power, virulent (and violent) socialism, anti-semitism, and atheism. Hitler simply did what Lenin preached; that is, set up a corporate state with the industries left in place, but doing the work of their socialist bosses.

A long-forgotten fact, a key to the understanding of Soviet history, is that Lenin and Trotsky were not Mensheviks; they were not Bolsheviks; in fact, THEY WEREN'T EVEN COMMU-NISTS. They were National Socialists, NAZIS, pure and simple. Hitler was still sucking his thumb when Lenin was first pushing the Nazi idea of capitalism managed by the state.

The ostensible "turn to capitalism" that we are witnessing today is not the first such move by the communist hierarchy. Lenin was smart enough to know that he couldn't just wipe out the entire capitalistic market structure that had developed under Czar Nicholas II and expect the country to get anywhere. Lenin urged upon his followers national socialism: capitalism with its expert managers under the control of the "socialist" state.

In Russia's temporary turn to free enterprise in 1921, the so-called New Economic Plan, there was an interesting economic event that has been almost lost to history. To rescue the Russian economy, the Bolsheviks turned to *gold*. They produced the chervonet, a solid gold coin to be used in international trade. (Private citizens in Russia were forbidden to own the chervonet; the penalty for disobedience was death.)

The gold-backed chervonet was accepted with enthusiasm all over the world. Four years after its introduction, it was worth MORE THAN THE DOLLAR. This is hard to believe, but true.

The communists, being the most economically moronic people on earth, just couldn't tolerate this symbol of the despised capitalist system, the chervonet, existing alongside the noble worker's ruble. The chervonet was discarded along with the New Economic Plan in 1928 and the communist experiment with economic sanity came to an end.

By 1990, socialist mismanagement had again brought the country to a state of near-coma, and so again there has been a turn to capitalism. This temporary return to reality is much more grandiose than the one in 1921, but I wonder if peristroika, just like the New Economic Plan before it, won't ultimately be revealed as just a pause, to permit yet another capitalist refuelling from the West.

Professor Richard Pipes, in his history of the Russian revolution, remarked on the completely hypocritical turn to a free market economy in the 1921 New Economic Plan:

> ...the government would retain a monopoly on political power but allow private enterprise a limited role in restoring the country's productive forces.... *once productivity had been sufficiently improved and the personnel stood available, a fresh offensive would be launched to exterminate the "bourgeois" class enemy for good and then to proceed in earnest with the construction of socialism.* [Emphasis added.]

This is precisely what happened. The country soon returned to its socialist straight-jacket and the mass murder of its citizens. Lenin missed his opportunity to beat the Nazis to the world's first corporate state. Boris Yeltsin (or his successor) may be more successful.

The Russian people seem even more foolish than Westerners in their reaction to this charade. They joke openly about the so-called decline of the KGB, yet an astonishing number of them support Yeltsin, who couldn't last five minutes as president of Russia without the support of the KGB, or the SSS, or the Russian Security Ministry, or whatever else it chooses to call itself. (I wish they'd go back to their original name, Cheka; it has a nice ring to it, don't you think?)

The difficulty of change in Russia is illustrated by an election in the Moscow area in the fall of 1992. The candidates fought each other savagely. They denounced the government, the bureaucracy, the mafia, business, and each other. They promised good times with sausage in every pantry, cheap bread, and cocoa for the kids.

The outcome? NOBODY was elected, because the minimum of 75 percent of the voters didn't show up. But, come to think of it, if we had such a democratic law, no one would get elected in the United States, either — and most of the time, that would be an improvement.

Some say the seemingly inexplicable support of the people for Yeltsin, in spite of the obvious fact that he has made matters worse, is due to the strong propensity for masochism and self-destruction in the Russian character. Ivan Bunin, a Russian writer, concluded that a Russian is unique in his lifelong quest to ruin himself by drink, gluttony, and self-inflicted misery. Russians find solace in their suffering, Bunin wrote. They like to have problems that they can "overcome." Could that be it?

There is the stereotype of the Russian woman, especially in the countryside, who expects to be beaten by her husband once a week. If he stops beating her, it means he doesn't love her anymore. This masochism is as old as Russia itself.

My pal Anatoly says that fully one-quarter of the population of Russia is psychotic. Maybe he's right; maybe the fundamental problem here is that 25 percent of the people are NUTS.

That may explain the growing power of Validimir Zhirinovsky. He is the leader of the "Liberal Democratic Party" (LDP), a group which is neither liberal nor democratic. Zhirinovsky is a true neo-Nazi. The LDP party newspaper carries glowing articles about Nazi theory; Zhirinovsky has links with the German Nazis; he's also buddies with Saddam Hussein. Watch out for him.

The death of communism

There is a disturbing complacency in the West concerning the "demise of communism." The collective thought process goes like this: Communism collapsed under the weight of its own incompetence and the unworkability of the planned socialist state. We won the Cold War. Now, everything's bound to get better.

So what if some old-line Bolsheviks are still around? Everybody knows that it will be impossible to go back to the old autocracy disguised as a "worker's and peasant's democracy." And modern communications make it impossible for a minority to take over the government as the Bolsheviks did in 1917. The attempted coup against Yeltsin proves this.

Besides, I've heard some pundits declaim, the "international community" and the force of moral public opinion worldwide would not put up with the reinstitution of a communist dictatorship.

I'm here to tell you that this reasoning is sophomoric and unrealistic. It is not based on the reality of Russian politics or the impotence of international organizations.

Russians know that communism doesn't work — but they have ALWAYS known this. People don't choose communism, it is always and everywhere IMPOSED on them.

Those who think the communists are merely an irritant and represent no threat to the semi-democracy now extant in Russia simply don't know what is going on. THE COMMUNISTS ARE TODAY IN A MUCH STRONGER POSITION THAN LENIN AND HIS LITTLE BAND OF PSYCHOTICS WERE JUST 48 HOURS BEFORE THEY SEIZED POWER IN A COUP D'ÉTAT.

The free press in Russia (and it truly is free, at least at this time) is warning the people of the obvious parallels between October 1917 and now. Mikhail Berger, a discerning columnist for the *Moscow Times*, said it in print: "The danger of a communist resurgence is becoming a reality."

The Communist Party of the Russian Federation and the Russian Communist Workers' Party have been resurrected and are both doing well. All of these far-left/far-right organizations, like the LDP and the various communist parties, are said to be on the fringe of Russian politics. But remember, Hitler was on the fringe when he started; so was Lenin.

Another rising star among the psychos of Russian politics is Nina Andreeva. Watch for that name. Nina has a massive head and the beefy, peasant face of a classic communist killer. She is creating her own Leninist-Stalinist political party and claims 50,000 members. She says she is going to overthrow the treasonous Yeltsin, who is nothing but a tool of "the international bourgeois." The fact that she was an informant for the KGB when at the Leningrad Institute does not bother her followers because, you see, that means she has always struggled for "Leninist ideals."

If you compare the Russia of October 1917 with the Russia of today, it is quite disturbing. The Bolsheviks were a tiny, despised group — even the other communists, and all the intellectuals who wanted a representative democracy, hated them.

If the Cold War is really over, why are all men at the age of 18 being drafted into the army? If communism is dead, then how do you explain the following? I was walking alongside the Winter Palace on a cold and rainy late-June afternoon (that's right, late June and definitely cold) when two open army trucks, both filled with soldiers, stopped for the traffic light. To my astonishment, the soldiers in the second truck were waving a large flag of the Soviet Red Army. It was the red flag of the communist Soviet Union, complete with the hammer and sickle, *not* the flag of the Russian Republic. I stopped and stared.

Their reaction to this glaring and obviously disapproving American (I was wearing a Confederate Army calvary officer's hat at the time, so they knew I wasn't one of them) was very interesting. They immediately hid the flag and began making lewd hand gestures toward me. As I could speak *that* language, I returned the same to them. Happily, no one jumped off the truck and came after me. The light changed and, as the trucks roared off, several of the soldiers gave me the old communist clinched-fist salute.

Is communism dead? As Mark Twain once said about stories of his own death, I'm afraid that reports of its demise have been greatly exaggerated.

Chapter Twenty-Three

Dodge City, Russia

Russia's history has been one of near-constant terror, interspersed with only brief periods of relative calm. The Tartar invaders terrorized the Russian empire for hundreds of years. The czars, including their beloved Alexander Nevsky, the Prince of Novgorod, collaborated with the Tarters to keep the people in a state of terror.

After the Tartars left, the terror continued as standard government policy. The czars had learned well from their masters. And of course, terror begets terror. In 1905 and 1906 terrorists killed and maimed 4,500 officials in the Russian empire. Adding private persons to the total of victims of left-wing terror, 9,000 souls fell to terrorism in those two years.

The history of Russia is replete with savage acts against government officials. Czar Alexander II was pulverized by two bombs as he stepped down from his carriage. Peter Stolpin, the closest thing to a statesman Russia has had, was shot and killed at a reception. Yes, terrorism has a long tradition in Russia.

At the beginning of the Age of Peristroika, terrorism abated a bit. But it is now resurging, as it always has in Russia. And some of the threats are for pretty big stakes: There have been repeated threats to blow up the nuclear power facility at Smolensk, for example. It's a mere 250 kilometers (and up wind) from the ten million people of Moscow. In 1991, there were

1,500 terrorist acts reported in Russia. There were over 100 bomb assassinations, with only 24 arrests.

One reason there are few apprehensions is because of the state's attitude toward, and definition of, terrorist acts. The Criminal Code of the Russian Federation only defines an act as "terrorist" if it was "the murder of a statesman or a public figure" and was done with the "aim of undermining Soviet power."

As in any police state, the only important crimes here are those against the authority of the state; crimes against the people are of no consequence.

This Russian disregard for the welfare and protection of its own citizens has been the case for centuries, whether under czarist absolutism, communist "neo-czarism," or today's bureaucratic dictatorship.

Here is how George Frost Kennan described the repressive regime of Alexander III:

> [T]o injure a portrait, statue, bust, or other representation of the czar set up in a public place is a more grievous crime than to assault and injure a private citizen as to deprive him of eyes, tongue, an arm, a leg or the sense of hearing.
>
> The mere concealment of a person who has formed an evil design [against the czar] ... is a more serious matter than the premeditated murder of one's own mother.... The private citizen who makes or circulates a caricature of the Sacred Person of the czar for the purpose of creating disrespect ... commits a more heinous crime than the jailer who [rapes] a ... defenseless girl 15 years of age.

Believe me when I tell you that things haven't changed much. During my last visit to St. Petersburg, a drunk driver plowed into a group of people at a bus stop. Three were killed, six more were hospitalized.

What will happen to the driver? He'll probably have his license suspended for six months (if he even *has* a driver's license, which is doubtful). No matter; he'll continue driving anyway. It's no big deal. Everybody gets drunk in Russia and these things happen. After all, it wasn't as though he had committed a crime against the state!

In June 1993, as I was getting ready to move out of this mad country, two trucks collided in a suburb of Moscow, one of them loaded with gasoline. There were three trolley buses alongside the accident scene. Russian trolley buses are almost always so packed that the doors have to be forced closed. The gasoline truck exploded and incinerated the nearest bus and all its screaming passengers. The scene was so ghastly that spectators at the site went into shock; many fainted.

Undoubtedly, one (or perhaps both) of the truck drivers was drunk. And just as undoubtedly, he will never serve a day in jail for his crime. In fact, I doubt if he was arrested.

We're getting almost as bad

Unfortunately, this attitude that the-only-serious-crime-is-a-crime-against-the-state now seems to have infected the United States. Killers, bank robbers, rapists, and other assorted offal will serve less time in jail than someone accused of cheating on his taxes.

Am I being too harsh? No, I'm being *too kind*. The truth is that, for the most brutal crimes in our country, no one is even arrested, much less sent to jail.

And even when a known vicious criminal *is* apprehended by the police, the authorities know the judge is likely to be a political hack and the ACLU will make sure all of the thug's "rights" are carefully protected.

Shakespeare had it wrong. Forget the lawyers — first, kill the *judges*. Or, if you want to be more civilized about it, join the Fully Informed Jury Association and help emasculate these black-robed emperors. (Call 1-800-TEL-JURY.) Having a sweet and forgiving nature, I recommend the latter. Besides, you might kill a few of the really good judges out there, who are as much prisoners of the present venal and unjust system as we are.

If the same killer or rapist mentioned above were to object to the graduated income tax on constitutional grounds, then he'd *really* be in trouble. His bank accounts would be frozen, his home and business padlocked, and his other assets seized. He will not only go to jail, he will also, for having perpetrated this heinous crime against the state, lose his God-given rights as an American citizen. He will not be allowed to vote or carry a gun.

This is not, it should be emphasized, for income tax *evasion*, for which you may or may not go to jail, but simply for challenging the authorities. But let me also point out that in most civilized countries, even evasion of taxes is not a felony but a misdemeanor for which no one goes to jail. If you get caught, you pay the taxes and a fine.

It's frightening to have witnessed, over the past 50 years, our decline into a bureaucratic oligarchy where crimes against the state are dealt with more seriously than crimes against citizens.

Private armies everywhere

But no matter how hard liberals try to reduce us to Russia's unhappy level, it is unlikely we will reach their standards of chaos and near-anarchy for many years, if ever.

Russia today contains a large number of armies, most of them with allegiance to no one but their leader. There are armies for political parties; there are armies for companies and churches; there are armies for individual politicians; there are armies for hire to any group with hard currency — and there is the *real* army, which is mostly composed of drunken, frustrated Russian officers and men who long for a return to the heady days of the Cold War. Most of these men are also for hire. In fact, if the price is right, you can even buy their uniform right off their backs, even in the dead of winter. I paid $60 for mine, including a great coat that must weigh 12 pounds.

Many of these "armies" in Russia may contain as few as six to a dozen men, but the number of actual *uniformed* armed groups is amazing. The Moscow Cossacks are a typical example of the not-so-raw material available with the potential to start an old-fashioned shoot-out that would make the OK Corral look like a church picnic.

The Cossacks are 650-men strong. They wear snappy uniforms complete with sabres — "just for show," says Georgi Kokunko of the Moscow Association of Cossacks. The Don Cossacks, from the Don River region, have two divisions of eight regiments and are exchanging grain for combat vehicles.

Troops of the Pamyat movement wear black uniforms, high boots, and shoulder belts reminiscent of the Nazi era. (In true Nazi fashion, they recently raided the offices of a local newspaper.) The leader of this "national patriotic front," Dmitry Vasilyev, is a state employee. He is the commissar at the Teremok agricultural cooperative, where he trains his soldiers.

The Russian National Legion contains 500 or more potential combatants. It is the private army of the National Republican Party of Russia. The legion has "no weapons," claims their leader, Sergei Maltsev. This being the case, one wonders how they managed to take part in combat operations in Trans-Dniestra and Tskhinval. Maybe they marched with broom handles, but I doubt it.

At least 18 men from this "legion" are fighting with those nice people, the Serbs, in the Yugoslav war of ethnic cleansing. Soon they'll be back in Russia, and Maltsev says with great enthusiasm: "Twenty well-trained men can give Moscow hell."

He added that these volunteers, who are very big on "slavic brotherhood ... are eager to spot a U.S. soldier through a gun sight." It all sounds uncannily like a replay of the beginning of World War I, when Russia came to the aid of Serbia in response to the threats of Kaiser Wilhelm.

The Liberal Democratic Party of Russia (LDPR) has its Falcons, consisting of 300 young men. This "youth organization" of the LDPR party wears pistol holsters as an "element of clothing." All of this has nothing to do with war, their commandant reassures us. But, he observes, "it is still better that the boys are already in uniform and with holsters if a civil war breaks out."

The "defenders of the White House," left over from the historic coup attempt, call themselves the August-91 and have a thousand members who wear spotless fatigues. Their commander says: "We are ready to defend democracy in any situation."

There is a new group, called the Army for Socialism, that has been passing out leaflets urging people to join their "military organization."

Even the Russian Professional Boxing League has gone military. They bought a children's summer camp and turned it into an arms training center. A raid revealed hand grenades, bullet-proof vests, and plenty of ammunition. I wouldn't be surprised if the St. Petersburg Garden Club became just as militant. They could ally with homosexuals and call themselves the St. Petersburg Pansy Division.

I just hope that when the crossfire starts, I'll be out of the country on business. Or at least bending over to tie my shoes.

Why not arm *everyone?*

The only good news is that there are plenty of weapons in the hands of peaceful citizens. I've seen estimates that the total number of guns in private hands in the entire old USSR is 30 million. Not enough, to be sure. But it's a start.

In Estonia, where they think the only good Russian is a dead Russian, a special decree by the government gives each resident the right to buy firearms for personal use. They only have to declare that the gun is being bought "for the protection of life and property." They're obviously smarter than we are — but they learned the hard way.

The leader of the Working Russia Movement, another neo-communist group, has an interesting concept on how to maintain a democratic press:

> A unified anti-fascist bloc will expose the true face of the current traitorous government hiding behind the mask of liberal-bourgeois democracy. We will draw up lists of the most fascist-minded journalists and, when we come to power, they will be shot.

Keep in mind that the term "fascist" hasn't the same meaning in Russia as it did when the communists were exhorting the people to give their last drop of blood in the great anti-fascist war. In the Russia of today, "fascist" simply means those in power. Even the new Nazi parties, which are springing up at an alarming rate, call the Yeltsin government "fascist."

The new Nazi wing of what can best be described as "communazis" is as alarming as the communist wing — and deadly serious. Russian National Unity (RNU) claims 40,000 members and their party head, Alexander Barkashov, boasts, "We have our people in the parliament, the ministry of the interior, and the KGB." I'm sure they do. The RNU gives lectures on maintaining the purity of the Slav race, calls Yeltsin a "yid," and warns about an international Jewish conspiracy against Russia.

(I'd better finish this book and get out of here. I'm not Jewish, but remember — one of the first groups Hitler went after was the Seventh Day Adventists. I suspect that, like Hitler, the new communazis will be equal opportunity oppressors.)

The most frightening of these political armies is the People's Patriotic Party (PPP). It grew out of the Afghan war veterans, a group of humiliated, neglected, and very bitter young men. They are all seasoned in war and hardship — and are ready for some kind of vindication. They have over 100,000 members.

There seems to be no end to this proliferation of independent military combat groups, answerable to no one but their "party" or their leader. A General Sterligov has announced the formation of the Headquarters of People's Resistance. Meanwhile, across town Lieutenant-Colonel Terekhov is forming the People's Volunteer Squads.

And what about Bashkirskaya, an aspiring republic a few hundred kilometers east of Moscow? They want independence: they have oil, which means they have great potential wealth. When will they start (or buy) their own army? Bashkirskaya is 30 percent Tatar, a group known historically for its fierceness and brutality. They enslaved the Russians for hundreds of years and would probably like to do it again. They'd be a match for anything the Russians could throw against them; for one thing, they'd be sober — a condition most Russians try to avoid.

Recruits to the Russian National Unity party are given "military-patriotic education." You need to understand that in Russia these days, "patriotic" means nationalistic communism; a return to the war against capitalism and personal freedom; a return to the paternalism of Stalin and Khrushchev; a return to the path of socialism and stability; a return to hell.

Will General Sterligov fight it out with Lieutenant Colonel Terekhov for control of the so-called conservative communist/Muslim right? Will the winner then go at it with the army of the Russian National Unity Party? Will the Moscow Cossacks, who will fight for anybody, join forces with the 100,000-strong PPP to eliminate Yeltsin's puny 1000-man August-91 army? Will the Russian National Legion bring back its broom-stick-wielding troops from Yugoslavia to join General Sterligov? After the "democratic" process has run its course, will there be any Russians left?

Democracy in action

Now, I am for every law-abiding citizen owning and carrying a gun. I think the way to end airline hijacking is to issue every adult passenger a 45-automatic when he or she enters the plane. But the Russian people are living among large groups of Kalashnikov-carrying drunks, idiots, fanatics, and would-be Stalins. I am opposed to gun control, but it seems to me a little armed-mob control is in order here.

Most of these groups claim to be ready to defend "democracy." But that word means different things to different groups — and almost never what it means to you or me. The communists (especially those in the West masquerading as liberals) have always described themselves as protectors of "democracy."

In trying to understand the Russian people, you must take all this hatred and insanity into consideration. You have to realize that the word "freedom" doesn't mean the same thing to a

Russian that it does to you and me. "Freedom" to a Russian means the KGB (or the State Security Service, as it's called now) is not torturing him, arresting his wife, or stealing his land.

In Russia you don't write a letter to your "representative" and tell him you think he is a dirty, rotten S.O.B. and that you not only won't vote for him, you're going to actively campaign for his opponent. Chances are, he really *is* a dirty, rotten S.O.B. He didn't get where he is by being a nice guy. And if he can, he'll use his influence to have you harassed, arrested, maybe even killed. It wouldn't be the first time.

I experienced this to a lesser degree when I was in the Navy. It never occurred to me that, just because I was in the military, I had lost my freedom to criticize my representatives in Washington. I was incensed with the way George Smathers, one of Florida's senators, was prostituting the office for his personal advantage.

I knew more about him than the local papers were willing to print — including one of his mistresses and some truly criminal financial shenanigans in Puerto Rico from which he'd profited handsomely.

His response was to bring pressure through the military to shut me up. He accused me of "inappropriate political activity," just because I'd called him a crook and a whore — which we both knew he was.

Now just imagine what would happen to a Russian, who has never experienced political freedom, writing to a "former" communist and telling him he is going to work against him. All I got in retaliation was a fitness report "with prejudice" (which means we don't like what you've done but we're not going to tell you why) and an IRS investigation. The dissenting Russian could meet with a fatal accident.

You must remember, *there is no representative government in Russia today*, no matter what you read in the U.S. press. Of that I can absolutely guarantee you.

Chapter Twenty-Four

Is Russia Really
Open for Business?

Luckily for me, I didn't come to Russia to find business deals. I came strictly (well, sort of strictly) for medical reasons: to learn as much as I could about photoluminescent therapy.

But like most Americans, I believed there were some truly remarkable economic opportunities here, and I told friends back home I'd be looking for the best of the bunch. The U.S. media had been bombarding us with propaganda about how Russia and Eastern Europe are "open for business."

Believe me, it's not true. Open for corruption, yes. Open for government interference, yes. Open for exploitation by World Bank bureaucrats, of course. But open for business? Barely.

Communism does not die easily. Nor does more than seven decades of dependency on Big Brother. The awful legacy of communism won't be changed in a day, a week, or a decade. It may never change. What the future holds for these people, both economically and politically, God only knows. I'm not a betting man, but if I were, I'd wager on a military coup and a return to the days of the Five Year Plan.

I hadn't been in St. Petersburg long before I started hearing horror stories about American and European businesses trying to work with Russians on various joint ventures. The stories I heard were a far cry from the glowing reports I'd read from the U.S.

Department of Commerce. To hear our government tell it, doing business in Russia was a snap. The Commerce Department even publishes a monthly newsletter to outline all of the opportunities that abound here.

The truth is a lot bleaker — tales of government interference, bribery, and shysterism of the very worst sort are commonplace. A friend from Texas told me the story of a recent attempt by a Texas oil man to "do a deal" with the Russians. An expert in drilling and retrieving oil, he'd show them how to get the oil flowing, thereby creating more wealth for them than they could imagine.

In the typical wasteful Soviet manner, 20 percent of the oil extracted here is spilled out of leaky pipes and cracked storage tanks. The total wastage in this incredibly inefficient country amounts to *more than Kuwait's pre-Gulf War production.*

Imagine how wealthy this country could be if it could only free *this one industry* from the shackles of socialism. But it doesn't work that way; the whole system needs to be jettisoned. And let me add that foreign aid, still considered the magic potion for ailing socialist economies, won't solve the problem. On the contrary, it will only encourage *more* waste and *more* suffering.

Where will investors be found who will put up a trillion and a half dollars a year to save these confused people? You won't see it in your lifetime. Once the world's largest oil producer, Russia will probably be an *importer* of oil by the time you read this. One oil man tried to make changes; here's what happened to him.

The deal was an uncomplicated joint venture. The Russians wouldn't have to risk a dime but would get half the profits. The Texan would put up all the cash, all the knowledge, and all the expertise. For that, he'd receive the other 50 percent of profits.

The papers were signed and the all-important Russian seals were affixed. Then the bureaucrats' greed glands kicked in. Billions of dollars would soon be gushing out of the ground — why should the Americans get *half?* They changed their minds and demanded that the contract be changed to a 60-40 deal in their favor.

The man from Texas was disgusted that the Russians had broken the contract before the ink on it had dried. But he figured he'd come thus far, he'd give up another 10 percent to keep the deal from collapsing.

The next day, as he was packing to return to Dallas, a committee representative called him at his hotel. The committee had changed its mind again and now insisted on receiving *80* percent of the profits. Forty percent for the Americans amounted to exploitation of the Russian people, they said.

Finally fed up, the oil man told them they could "go to the south 40" (or something like that), and headed for home. The committee panicked and met him en mass at the airport. "Forty percent would be fine," they said. "Even 50 percent. Please don't go."

It doesn't take a successful businessman long to figure out it would be 50 percent today, 30 percent tomorrow, and nothing the day after that.

Two more examples

Perhaps the Texas oil man heard about Sandy Swanson and his fishing deal with the Russians. Sandy is a successful businessman from Seattle, Washington. He entered into a contract with a former fishing cooperative at the far eastern port of Khabaroysk. The Americans eventually had to come up with all the supplies, such as boats, fuel, ice, and bait, because the Russians did not put up their part of the deal.

In spite of this bad start, Swanson decided to go ahead with the project and give the Russians half of net profits: a good deal for the Russians, as they had nothing invested, and certainly a good deal for the Russian government that would rake in 26 percent of the market value of the fish before they would allow them to be exported. There would also be a 32 percent tax on profits and all employees would get slapped with a 40 percent income tax. Then there are local taxes and "fishing quota fees," which are calculated, not by the ton as in saner climes, but by *counting the individual fish.*

Determined not to quit, Swanson's people went to sea and brought back several tons of fish. The catch was worth about $600,000 on the world market. This "easy money" so dazzled the authorities that they demanded another $156,000 on top of the other taxes.

The math went something like this: 26 percent off the top would be $156,000. Add another $156,000, and you owe the state $312,000. With Swanson's own expenses of $300,000, the bills came to $12,000 more than the market value of the catch — and that was before he paid to have each fish counted!

But these losses are peanuts compared to those of the Moscow Lamp Factory and its British partner, the Moscow International Electronic Center (MIEC). The Brits of MIEC had what looked like a dream deal: They took a standard ramshackle building that had experienced 26 years of socialist neglect and turned it into a beautiful, capitalistic symbol of the new economic order coming to a freedom-starved Russian populace.

Five companies employing 400 people quickly moved in. Xerox, Ferguson Holly Agency of London, and the European Broadcast Union signed up as tenants.

The renovation cost the company 350 million rubles, but it looked like a solid investment — blue chip companies were moving in, the company's telephone-assembly business was doing well, and that born-again capitalist, Boris Yeltsin, would be their great Russian bear, ready to protect all his little capitalistic cubs.

But then the bear turned on his young. Yeltsin decreed that MIEC and its Russian partner, the Moscow Lamp Factory, be evicted from the building. What's more, he ordered that all the contents (including 200 international telephone lines, five telex lines, and 4,000 local phone lines) be turned over to the state.

To make sure there was no misunderstanding, riot police were sent in to give MIEC the heave-ho. A dismayed Samuel Osman, president of MIEC, said he didn't understand the grounds for the decree. It's very simple, Sam. Once a project approaches fruition, the Russians have a bad habit of not keeping their word. I can hear their arguments now: Why should a bunch of *foreigners* occupy that beautiful building? It belongs to *all* of the people. Take it back!

The naive Mr. Osman learned a bitter lesson: "There is no law in Russia today. They talk about foreign investment and at the same time, they are pushing everyone out."

Moscow officials break a deal

The saga of the Ducat-Liggett cigarette joint venture should cool the ardor of anyone dreaming of making millions in the former Soviet Union. Forget the fact that you don't like cigarettes — this case could just as easily have been a baby-food operation — and consider the preposterousness of the business climate in "capitalist" Russia.

The American investors, the Liggett part of the name, made a deal with the Ducat cigarette factory in Moscow. The Americans would improve the quality of the cigarettes, which were little more than roasted weeds and dirty rags (machine parts were often found in tobacco bales — it boosts your profits when you're paid by the kilogram), and they would greatly increase production. This was a joint venture with the city of Moscow, which had only to supply the business with the existing, essentially worthless factory.

Liggett put up a cool $7 million for a new office complex and $700,000 as a capital contribution. This did not include the many millions they would have to spend on the construction of a brand-new, state-of-the-art tobacco factory.

The company learned that the factory director was, in the usual Soviet fashion, stealing money from the company. This was discovered by a method the manager had never heard of: an audit. He was not impressed by this thing called an audit as he, the director, was entitled to steal as much as he needed to maintain his nomenklatur lifestyle.

When the company fired him, he refused to leave his office and posted guards at the factory to keep "nosey" officials away. A worker was beaten nearly to death and a journalist received death threats. Now, get this: So far, city officials in Moscow have taken no further action against the manager. In fact, they have destroyed the entire project by invalidating the land and property leases of the company.

While the business goes up in smoke, and Liggett is out several million dollars, the bureaucrats of the city council loose nothing. The real losers are the people of Russia, as confidence in doing business in Russia continues to erode.

The Japanese, for example, are fleeing as fast as decorum will permit. While they had a yen to do business with their former enemy, it just wasn't worth the trouble or risk when investment opportunities were so fabulous in their own backyard.

Bring your own workers

If on-going battles with your "partner," the government, aren't reason enough to discourage foreign investment here, then there is also the all-pervasive corruption and, perhaps the most frustrating of all, the general incompetence of the labor force.

Andrei Malgin, the gloomy editor of the weekly Russian news magazine, *Stolitsa*, relates the story of a company that hired a Russian worker to do the simple task of moving a computer from one room to another. Why hire expensive imported European labor for such a simple job when there is a Russian worker on the floor below, working for a German-Russian firm, who will do the simple task for a few rubles?

It was a very costly decision. There was a wire connecting the computer to some other things. Instead of disconnecting it, he took some scissors and cut it. There was a grand flash of light and a lot of very bad sounds from mortally wounded computers, printers, fax machines, and telecommunications equipment. Everything quit. The link to the satellite was lost. But worst of all, the computers crashed, losing all their priceless stored data. It took a month of desperate damage control — after shipping in experts from Washington, Munich, and Vienna — before everything was up and running again.

Malgin, an educated and sincere Russian, concludes laconically: "I do not want to say that Russians are idiots and bunglers. That would be unpatriotic. I love my people. But they are not yet ready to work in a civilized country. For this reason my advice to foreign entrepreneurs is: Bring everything you need with you, including workers."

Let's import some lettuce

You still want to do business in Russia? Well, then, I have an idea for you. There is no lettuce in Russia. There hasn't been any since the Great October Socialist Revolution in 1917. There's plenty of kapusta (cabbage), but no lettuce.

You say to the commissar — excuse me, my mistake — Director of Vegetable Imports: "I want to import lettuce. How much tax will I have to pay?"

"It depends," he replies.

"Depends on what?"

"A lot of things," he helpfully explains.

"Well, let me rephrase the question. Can you give me an estimate of the tax I will have to pay on my profits?"

He studies the ceiling. "Forty percent," he replies with enthusiasm, having apparently discovered this figure under the peeling ceiling paint.

"Forty percent of the profits?"

"No," he replies indignantly, "forty percent of the price you charge. How do *we* know how much profit you're making?"

You attempt to reason with him: "It's expensive to ship fresh lettuce to Russia. We anticipate our profit will only be 20 percent. With a 40 percent tax, we'll lose 20 percent."

He folds his arms; his big moment has arrived: "Then maybe importing lettuce isn't good business for you — heh, heh, heh."

Very funny.

"Besides," he adds as you are heading for the door, "Russians don't need lettuce; they have plenty of kapusta."

And therein lies the heart of the problem. As the bureaucrat in control of vegetable imports, he has total control over deciding what the Russian people *need*. What they *want* is entirely irrelevant to him. In fact, the idea that they should *freely choose,* by paying money through the marketplace, he views as dangerous and, yes, even evil.

Still interested in doing business here? First let me talk to you about a bridge I have for sale in Tashkent.

Chapter Twenty-Five

Detours on the Road to Capitalism

Each day I see firsthand how difficult, if not impossible, it will be to turn these people, this city, and this country into a haven for capitalism. Russia is a country based on the serf mentality. No matter how much money the world pumps into this economy (and the West is wasting *billions* on this, as I'll show you in a moment), I'm afraid that mentality will remain.

It's not the fault of the Russian people. The serfs were enslaved by the monarchy for most of Russia's history. It wasn't until 1861 that Alexander the Liberator freed them, and that freedom was very short-lived. Less than 60 years later, the communists had taken over and enslaved everyone.

Like the Russian serfs, the new Russian man — the hero of the Revolution — lived in a commune. The communist master was the judge, the jury, and the executioner. Like the serf, the new Russian man was told where to work and how to work; neither the serf nor the communist citizen could own property. Nothing had really changed.

The only way to fight the system was to develop a layer of cunning and duplicity: tell "the man" what he wanted to hear, believe nothing, and expect nothing. Cynicism and stoicism were essential for survival, while initiative and independent thinking were a sure route to the gulag — or worse.

This mentality makes sense for the serf and the man enslaved by communism, but it doesn't work in a capitalist system.

Unfortunately, the Russian of today has brought his deceit to the world of capitalism. The results are catastrophic for Russia and for the poor suckers from the West. Until they learn to respect contracts in Russia, capitalism cannot take root. The western capitalist will come; he will look; he will experience a few bad deals; and he will leave, taking his skills and know-how with him.

There was a survey taken among a group of state enterprises in St. Petersburg about their attitudes toward the free market. The conclusion? The overwhelming majority said it was a system whereby "devious and cunning people take advantage of the modest and honest." Less than one in four thought that initiative and enterprise should merit any "extra" reward. The Russian peasant comes from a thousand-year history of living under a system of communal agriculture. It goes back long before the word "communism" was invented.

But it's not just the peasant. Only about one person in four in this crazy city makes any attempt to better himself or herself by earning extra income. Although desperate for more goods, they won't *earn* them. They prefer to do things the old way: complain and look vainly to the all-powerful state for rescue.

It's a collective father complex. The cold and humorless Lenin, even though he seized power through terror and with practically no popular support, metamorphosed into "Grandfather Lenin" and so quickly replaced the Tzar as the collective father. The vast majority of Russians honestly believe that people are the children of the state and *must* be provided with housing, education, entertainment, a job, food, and health care (and vodka).

With this social infantilism, and the childish expectations generated from it, it is no wonder they blame "capitalism," which they have not really tried, for their present economic hardship. (Reminds you of our own "liberals," doesn't it?) With their lack of political sophistication, it would be just as easy for the West to become their new father figure and the source of all good and wonderful things — distributed equally, of course, to all of Russia's 300 million children.

I saw a newspaper poll where Russians were asked to describe the most outstanding characteristics of Western and Russian business people. Westerners were most often described as having "high professionalism" and "practical sense." Russian business people, on the other hand, were described as having a "thirst for profit" and a "swindler's nature."

A Russian psychologist, Zarina Gorbaleva, says the idea of business ethics sounds like "a total contradiction to most people." (Incidentally, her first name certainly reflects a change: You wouldn't dare name your daughter "empress" in the old days!) And Vladimir Preobrazhensky, a Russian who is actually trying to run his business following Western principles, says, "In Russian, to call someone an 'idealist' means he is a fool."

I have had enough experience with Russia's grimy reality so that I'm no longer naive about how things work here. Most Russians believe it simply isn't possible to be honest and successful at the same time.

On the subject of bribes, there's another side to that story I should mention. A Russian traffic policeman, who makes less than $10 a month, says that it is the system itself that has forced him into corruption. "If I received a normal salary, I wouldn't take bribes," he claims. "But without taking bribes I wouldn't be able to feed my wife, who is pregnant. We do it in order to survive, not to play in the casino."

Things Russians *don't* need

All this chaos and corruption may be something that just has to be endured, as part of the metamorphosis of a socialist society into a capitalist one. Maybe we shouldn't be too critical of a people who have never experienced freedom — the freedom to buy and sell, the freedom to think and criticize, even the freedom to move from one place to another in their own country.

And I have to add, the duplicity, double-dealing, and sheer stupidity shown by many Russians (especially those in positions of authority) are equalled again and again by visitors from the West (especially those with government funds to spend). For every idiotic bureaucrat eager to destroy the first bloom of capitalism, there's a so-called western capitalist — with help from his own bureaucrats — ready to put the screws to as many poor Russians as possible.

Adding to the deprivation and other burdens of the Russian people are companies like Pepsi Cola. The president of Pepsi, David Jones, has been pushing his nutrition-free swill for years in communist countries, including working with the Butcher of Bucharest, Nicolae Ceausescu. Now he's joined Coke in deciding that Russia is where the action is.

Jones admits that his "as-yet-unborn grandchildren may be the first to see any profits from the company's ventures in Russia." I think he's being too optimistic. If you're a stockholder in Pepsi, you might ask management why Jones is investing hundreds of millions of dollars in Russia, with a payoff decades away (if ever), when there are hundreds of other, more stable markets available TODAY, not in the year 2030.

And you might also ask how guzzling Pepsi is going to help the impoverished people of Russia, who can't get fresh milk for their children and already suffer from nutritional anemia *without* the help of Pepsico.

Jones says, "This country has enormous potential." If he means lots of people who don't yet have a twelve-pack a week habit, he's right. Sadly, there are a lot of gullible people over here who can hardly wait to waste precious resources on liquid candy like Pepsi Cola. They want to be as much like Americans as possible.

But Jones, with his liquid govno, isn't the only "entrepreneur" sticking it to the Russians. Far from it. One of the biggest swindles are all the "consultant services" you and other taxpayers provide. You're paying $300 a day (that's a *year's salary* for the average Russian) to an endless stream of "consultants," "accountants," "investment bankers," and "educators" to come over here and deliver a lot of impractical advice that usually can't be acted upon. The teams of "experts" almost never include any Russians who could actually contribute something worthwhile.

There is little if any connection between what Russia needs and what these con artists "study" and, adding to the waste, costly investigations are often repeated by different foreign experts. One such boondoggle was the study of Russian seed potatoes. *Three different foreign agencies* did the same research, with each study costing hundreds of thousands of dollars. The money would have been much better spent on a few hundred thousand copies of Henry Hazlett's masterpiece, *Economics in One Lesson* — which most of these "consultants" undoubtedly haven't read.

And don't forget the loot raked in by the writers, designers, and printers of all the fancy (and useless) brochures that arrive in a never-ending cornucopia from the World Bank, the International Monetary Fund, the International Finance Corporation, and other governmental agencies, offices, and institutes. This costly junk lines the shelves of ministry officials, collects dust, and is seldom read.

But the biggest swindler of all has got to be the European Bank for Reconstruction and Development (EBRD). This government-financed boondoggle doesn't reconstruct and doesn't develop. What it DOES do is waste taxpayer's money. These plutocrats spent *millions* of dollars refurbishing their London offices before they'd committed a single dime to assist anyone or anything in Russia. Just their office Christmas party last year cost over $80,000!

The best thing that could ever happen to Russia is for all of these groups to run out of money. (And one of the best things that could ever happen to our country would be for the voters to finally wise up, and pull the plug on all of these profligate internationalists. I say, fire 'em all!)

The mafia goes international

Perhaps the greatest accomplishment of peristroika has been to unleash a new class of criminals on an unsuspecting world. The Russian mafia has invaded Western Europe, the United States, Africa, and Southeast Asia. And of course it is an extremely powerful presence in all the republics of the former Soviet empire.

These aren't the "deez" and "doze" boys of Brooklyn, by the way. For the most part, these gangsters have advanced degrees in science, engineering, or mathematics; they speak several languages fluently; and they can move in the most sophisticated and urbane settings.

Superior to the Cosa Nostra, the Russian mafiosi are smarter, meaner (according to law enforcement officials), more cunning and duplicitous, and have the distinct advantage of being able to use the services of "out-of-work" KGB agents to run their rackets and rub out people who get in the way.

You can easily spot the mafia leaders in Russia — they're the ones driving Mercedes and other expensive imported cars. No honest citizen here can afford a car. And you never see a woman driving a car here, either. It's an all-male Panzer attack on the pedestrians of the city. They love to roar up to a group of people crossing the street, slam on their brakes just before killing a half dozen of them, and — honking their horn all the while — nudge the people out of the way as if herding cattle.

These traffic terrorists are either powerful state bureaucrats or members of the criminal underground. Whichever they are, I don't much like them. So when conditions are right, I give them a good "kaluch job" as they go whizzing by. I take my house key, called a kaluch, and dig it into the paint of their ill-gotten Mercedes.

Although I sometimes feel a little camaraderie with the anti-tax-collector, anti-communist brigands who comprise the Russian mafia, the truth is they pose an awesome problem for law enforcement in Russia *and now in the West as well*. The break-up of the old Soviet Union was like exploding a giant colony of fire ants which have metastasized to most of the industrial nations in the world.

The accomplishments of the Russian-American mafia are awesome: They pulled off the largest jewelry heist, the largest insurance fraud, and the largest Medicare fraud in American history, netting over $1 billion from these crimes alone. They are alleged to have smuggled into the U.S. huge, radioactive poppies from the Chernobyl area. Won't *those* cause some interesting dreams!

And what is the West doing to defend itself against the invasion of the Russian mafia? Europol, the European Community's answer to organized crime in Europe, has five police officers in a hut in Strasbourg working on the problem. In Russian vernacular they would be described as paper pigs with no teeth. But I'm sure the hut has a good view of the Rhine River.

At least Russia has one advantage over Europe and the U.S. There are practically no bank robberies in Russia. This is because, according to General Chebotarev, head of the Russian Organized Crime Control Department, the mafia now owns and/or controls all the banks there. Isn't it comforting to know that if your typical Russian ever has any money to save (something that's extremely unlikely), he can trust the crooks who own the bank not to steal it from him!

Chapter Twenty-Six

Will She Love My Liver?

There was an AIDS conference in Turkey Nikolai needed to attend and he invited me to go with him. I accepted with alacrity; I'd never seen Istanbul before and wondered what it was like. Rather than spend two days on the incredibly unpleasant Russian trains, as poor Nikolai was required to do, I took the train to Helsinki and flew down from there. Being a "rich American" occasionally had its advantages!

I decided I'd bring back an attractive dress for Leda. I didn't know her size but, as I saw it, if I got it large enough, she would make it fit. Women have an uncanny way of doing this that no mere man could ever understand. They wear each other's clothes as if they were all the same size. It's much too mysterious for me.

Istanbul was a delightful surprise, a city of water and mosques, strange sounds and delicious, exotic foods. At the shopping center, I met an outstanding Turkish beauty: raven-black hair, coffee-and-cream skin, and deep blue eyes. Her name is Silhouette of the Moon (Aitule). She said, through my taxi driver-interpreter, that she wanted me to teach her English. As he was repeating her remarks, she looked first at my left eye, then at my right, rapidly moving her eyes back and forth. I don't know why some women do this, but I found it absolutely hypnotizing.

But Leda is all the English student I need (or can handle) at this point in my dissolute life. I wasn't really tempted anyway — my flight for Helsinki was leaving in two hours. Besides, my daughter Tracy has warned me about dating girls younger than my children. She says no good can come of it.

I had a little culture shock on my return to St. Petersburg. I walked into a moloko (milk) store a few blocks from my apartment and stepped into a two-foot-wide puddle of water. The ancient marble floor was covered with rivulets of mud. After two weeks in clean Turkey and immaculate Finland, I had forgotten that this disgusting mess is perfectly normal in this backward country.

The next day, I again forgot that I was in the land of the perpetual shortage and wandered into an apotek to purchase some bandages. To make sure the clerk didn't misunderstand my pigeon Russian, I had brought along my empty bandage box.

After a wait of no more than 30 or 40 minutes (it was a slow morning), I made it to the front of the line and showed my empty box to the harridan behind the counter.

She glanced at me, my box, shook her head, and said, "Nyet."

"When do you expect to have them in?" I asked.

She gave me her best what-a-stupid-question look and replied, "How should I know?"

It was clear that she was finished with me and wanted to abuse the next "customer" in the long line behind me. But I asked one more question: "When did you last *have* bandages here?"

"I don't remember, 1988, I think — WE DON'T HAVE ANY BANDAGES," she snarled and turned away to her next victim.

"I love you with all my liver"

The St. Petersburg nights are shortening, now that we are past the winter solstice. But for some strange reason, they seem even longer. I suppose it's because Leda is on vacation in Estonia with the hated Vladimir. (Yes, I finally found out what she meant by "friends." He's the dirty rotten Russian I'm trying to replace in her life.)

I didn't handle her disclosure very well. I was feeling more than a little desperate, so in the subway before she left, with a hundred or so people looking on at this strange American, I blurted out: "Leda, please give me two years of your life — you won't regret it. I love you with all my heart."

I spoke the last sentence in Russian. I thought she would be impressed with my language skills and would have no doubt as to my sincerity.

Her Russian grey eyes widened, the earth stopped for an interminable two seconds — and she burst out laughing.

Oh, the anguish! Oh, the crushing disappointment! In an instant, I had gone from impetuous young buck to a toad. I looked around, to see if I could slide under the doors or hide behind a seat.

But then she flushed and said, "Beel, I'm sorry. I didn't mean that the way it seemed." (I advanced from a frog to the status of a dog — a definite improvement.)

"You said, 'I love you with all my liver,' and I don't think you really meant that. Please don't be angry with me."

My heart started beating again. Later, we would laugh at my fractured Russian. This time, I switched to English, so there would be no misunderstanding.

"Leda, please. Give me two years of your life. I will make you very happy and you'll never regret it."

"Maybe one," she replied.

"A year and a half," I countered.

Done. I should have opened with five and settled for three.

A wonderful Russian night

The sexes here don't seem to like each other very much. It's obvious that Russian men don't know how to treat a woman. The women see the average Russian man as childish, drunken, and uncaring. The Russian male's attitude toward the opposite sex is a little simpler: the wife should be a cook, a housekeeper, and a sexual convenience. That's about it.

How could a man entertain such an attitude toward a lovely human being like Leda? And there are millions of Leda's out here, just waiting to be loved and protected. What a waste of some of the finest women on this earth.

We came home early from dinner one particularly cold and snowy night. I was still in the process of removing layer upon layer of her doubts and disappointments with men. I asked her if I could rub her back with a little oil. She seemed startled, as if I had asked her if I could burn her hair. But then she recovered and said, "Rub my back with oil? Well, yes, Beel."

I rubbed the satin contours of her back and cautiously moved onward. She seemed asleep, but she suddenly rolled over and pressed me firmly to her. Her head arched back, she mumbled something in Russian and exploded into another plane of consciousness that only a woman would understand.

The morning after this delicious St. Petersburg night, we confirmed our agreement that she would give me 18 months of her life. The hated Vladimir was history.

By March, there is a silver glow in the St. Petersburg sky until almost midnight. The korishka, the small silver fish that smell like cucumbers, are streaming down the Neva. It is a perfect time to be in love.

We are an unusual pair: me, a Scottish-American with over 200 years of American tradition in his family; she, the daughter of a retired Soviet army officer, born into a nation of terror and mind control in the dismal city of Vorkuta, well above the Arctic Circle. So little in common, yet feeling this immense attraction for each other.

But no matter how happy we are, no matter how passionate the declarations of love, there is a reserve in her I can't reach — some hidden access to her heart or mind that is closed and barricaded. There is a negativity in her, as there is in most Russians I know. We've never discussed it, but perhaps she thinks she *must* marry a Russian man, that it is somehow part of her destiny. Every Russian is incredibly fatalistic.

It is not that she is keeping deep, dark secrets from me. She is no KGB agent, of that I am certain. When I finally told her of my early suspicions, we laughed almost as much as we do when I say, "I love you with all my liver."

Then what is the problem? I don't know, and she won't discuss it with me. Certainly, 30 years of deprivation, communist terror, and constant fear has got to engender a little pessimism and strangeness in a beautiful, intelligent, and ambitious woman who sees nothing but bureaucratic vindictiveness, terrible tragedy, and mind-numbing poverty and chaos all around her.

"Come with me to Finland," I beg her. "You'll love Finland. And I will love showing it to you." (I had already decided to move to the port of Turku, on Finland's west coast, when I leave St. Petersburg.)

"That's impossible, Beel." She turned her head away.

"No, it's not," I replied. "Come live with me there. I'll have my writing and other work. I could even start a clinic for foreigners and you could be part of it."

I saw that familiar glint of diamond-hard stubbornness in her eyes. "I don't know anything about medicine," she said. "It's not possible. Let's talk about something else."

So we did.

Chapter Twenty-Seven

Music, Musings, and a Snake

The great Russian conductor, Mstislav Rostropovich, was expelled in disgrace from Russia in 1978 as "politically unreliable," essentially a traitor to the Soviet workers' state, and was stripped of his citizenship. He immigrated to America and became conductor of the National Symphony Orchestra.

In an action unprecedented in Russian history, he was invited back in 1990 and given a hero's welcome, not only by the people, but by the Russian government. On the arrival of Rostropovich and his family, there were hundreds of people at the Pulkova airport with signs reading, "Thank You for Solzhenitsyn," the greatest Russian writer of the 20th century who had defended Rostropovich, and "Welcome Home, Slava!" The word "Slava," as used here, has a double meaning: Slava is a nickname for Rostropovich's first name, Mstislav, and it is also a Russian term for unbounded respect, honor, and love. The czar of Russia and the Virgin Mary might both have been hailed with "Slava — honored art thou!"

The audience could hardly contain itself and tears ran down Rastropovich's cheeks during the entire performance. For the end of the concert, he chose two pieces to honor his adopted homeland. The orchestra played a piece by George Gershwin and, as a finale, the great Souza march, "Stars and Stripes Forever." The audience, clapping in unison, went wild.

After the performance, Sophia, the Queen of Spain, asked Rostropovich for his autograph. He signed, in a clever mixture of Russian and English, "To Her Majesty with love from your slave, Slava." After a night like that one, you can't help loving the Russian people and the Russian soul.

But, I must add that, although the reaction to Rostropovich was electric and moving, it was primarily a political reaction and not really a response to his music.

The average Russian is not interested in culture, such as opera, ballet, and the symphony. All of the great Russian composers may as well have never been born as far as he is concerned. My guardian seagull, Nikolai Chaika, said he has never seen one of his colleagues from the Pasteur Institute at a symphony or other cultural event. The communists didn't kill off all the artists, just most of the patrons.

Culture continues to exist today only because of a small, dedicated group of artists who are subsidized by the state. As a great pianist will only make $20 a month (while a props man will earn $25), subsidizing an orchestra or ballet is no great strain on the budget. Besides, it's good press, as well as a profitable tourist draw. A ticket to the opera is only a few cents for a Russian, but $40 for an American.

Greta and I used to spend a lot of time at the magnificent Russian concert halls and palaces that had their own theaters for concerts. Nikolai would buy the tickets. As a native, he could get the best seats in the house for less than a dime. For all the sacrifices I made in material comfort during my sojourn in Russia, this made up for a lot.

At a loss for words

Leda and I went to see "La Traviata" last night at one of St. Petersburg's exquisite theaters. I brought her three roses. You *never* give a lady an even number of flowers in Russia. You would reveal yourself to be a hopeless clod and vulgarian. As everyone knows, even numbers of flowers are only given at funerals.

At the concert, just as the prince's father was consoling his son on the tragic loss of his sweetheart, an alley cat strolled across the stage, oblivious to the great drama unfolding before him. He stopped, scratched his ear, and moved on.

There was a wave of subdued laughter from the audience as the performers pressed on. In the old days, the cat probably would have been shot — or at least exiled to Siberia.

After the performance, we went to the Artists' Cafe, our favorite spot for rubbing knees, listening to lovers' music (violin and piano softly playing Russian folk songs) and wishing, at least in my thoughts, that there wasn't so much in our lives that separated us. The conversation got around to my son.

"How old is he, Beel?"

"About 25," I replied. (You know you're *really* getting old when you lie, not only about your own age, but also the age of your children.)

I wanted to tell her how much she meant to me. How much I wanted her to share *all* of my life, here in St. Petersburg and afterward. How would I express it?

"Leda, I love every hair on your head, I love the very dollops of St. Petersburg mud on your boots."

No, that wouldn't do. Snoopy could do better than that. I remained mute.

Bitten by a snake

It's June now, and my St. Petersburg nights are coming to an end. Soon I will be leaving here. Where will I go? Will Leda come with me? When will I be back?

There were many questions, but few answers. So I went for a stroll through my favorite park. It was 10:00 p.m. and there was still so much daylight that people were reading newspapers on the park benches.

The park across from the Peter and Paul Fortress is one of my favorite places in the city. It has lovely trees, many family-type statues of children at play, statues of young girls thinking pensively about whatever young girls think about (I think I know, but I'm not sure), and statues of fully developed naked young men and women — thinking about politics, I'm sure.

There's a zoo of half-starved animals at the far end of the park; a prison really, rather than a zoo. It symbolizes this beautiful, decaying city to me. Beneath the veneer of awesome architecture is a much larger zoo: five million half-starved souls in the prison that used to be Leningrad.

I thought of the time, a few months earlier, when I'd seen a girl with a large python around her neck standing under a large shade tree in this same park. I told the girl I had a medical clinic in Africa (she feigned interest) and asked if the snake came from there. No, she said, the reptile was from Cuba.

She was with two men and they had a good business going, taking pictures of people draped with this seven-foot snake. I'd never had a picture taken with a python while I was in central Africa, although we ran over one once on the way to Kabale in southern Uganda. (Another time, a cobra was killed just outside the clinic door. At least they told me it was a cobra; for all I knew, it could have been a harmless garden snake.)

When I saw the Cuban python, I thought, what the heck?, I'll get a picture taken with this one. You wouldn't even know the picture was taken in Russia, not Africa, unless some mushik was standing behind me holding a vodka bottle. I told them to blur the background.

So I wanted to fake photographic history a bit. Is that so terrible? Am I losing my credibility here?

I agreed to pay two bucks — the special, eight-times-more-than-a-native price, just for wealthy foreigners — and they offered me a receipt promising delivery in six weeks. I made it clear to them I wasn't born yesterday. I showed them my subway pass. "See, I *live* here." They didn't understand my English, or pretended not to, but the pass made the message clear.

I gave them the address of the Pasteur Institute, thinking that my official connections would bring dark clouds of anxiety and fear to their brows, and deter them from ripping me off. Sometimes you have to play hard ball.

Apparently they weren't afraid of me or the Pasteur Institute. The photo of me bravely holding the python never arrived. Serves me right, you're probably saying.

The snake returns

A few weeks after these musings, I was at a typical Russian restaurant a few blocks from the park. I had promised to treat Nikolai, Galia, and Leda to a little zakuska, the Russian "starters" we all liked so much, plus vodka and dinner. This particular eatery has a group that plays a lot of Glenn Miller and we all got a little dreamy, listening to "Moonlight Serenade" and "Moonlight Cocktails." That music is certainly a lot more romantic that anything our children listen to these days.

We'd heard two or three songs when who should come into the restaurant but the snake charmers with my seven-foot friend. They asked if we would like to pose with the snake. (Leda moved as far away from it as she could.)

I explained to Nikolai how these rascals had already stripped me of two dollars and recommended we pass. Nikolai became a very aggressive seagull. He leapt from his chair and tore into the trio with some rather harsh Russian, all delivered *fortissimo*. (I could tell it was harsh from the expression on Leda's face.) The band stopped playing in the middle of "Stardust" and all faces turned in our direction.

The serpentine scammers made a quick recovery. They were new here, they explained. They had never seen me before and the snake had only arrived last week.

It looked like the same snake to me. "Where is the snake from?" I asked.

"Cuba," the girl replied.

Fearful that Nikolai would kill them — or worse yet, the snake — if I told him that part, I temporized. Maybe it was a different group, I said. And yes, the snake *did* look a little different from the one I'd posed with.

After a few moments, Nikolai quieted down and the band resumed playing.

I took Leda to the dance floor and held her as close as she would let me. I quickly forgot about my two-dollar loss.

Afterwards I invited Leda back to my apartment for drinks.

"No, Beel, you know I have to get up early tomorrow."

Why are women always on a different schedule? Or maybe it was just an excuse. Maybe Leda is getting tired of me. Still, it was a great evening.

Chapter Twenty-Eight

The Summer Solstice

Summer has finally arrived in St. Petersburg and has pushed away the uncertainty of the St. Petersburg spring. With June comes the inundation of the city by millions of delicate, cotton-like balls of the topol tree. This botanical sexual excess is the result of the union of the male and female topol.

These zygotes of sex-without-pleasure vary in size from a pin head (and even smaller) to the dimensions of a small grape. They float up, down, and sideways, looking for a place to take root and germinate during the long St. Petersburg winter nights.

Perverse man, or I should say perverse boy, can turn this sensual expression of nature into a disaster. At the height of its spawning frenzy, the pollen can cover a city street. Boys have discovered that if you put a match to it, a flash fire will sweep the area, sometimes igniting oil, wood, gasoline — and even people.

I was away from this city of grandeur and squalor for most of the birth pains it endures every year at this time, a time of hopeful parturition to sun and warmth. But I arrived back in time to enjoy those nurturing rays that most of us take for granted, but often elude you here in the far north.

It's been almost a year since I arrived on that inopportune Sunday, lost in a world that carried me back to my childhood of the depression years in Georgia. There I could speak the language and had Mom, Grandma Lucy, and Uncle John to guide and protect me. Here, except for my protective seagull, I was alone. It's hard to believe you can feel like a child when you are yourself a grandfather, but I learned it's possible ... and it's not fun.

"The more things change..."

Continuing my boycott of Aeroflot, I took Sibelius, the fast Finnish train, from Helsinki to St. Petersburg. As always, it was clean, efficient, safe, and it slid into St. Pete precisely on schedule. While we travelled, I thought back to my first train trip into Russia from Latvia; it was one-third as fast, ten times as dangerous, and about a thousand times less clean.

I remembered my arrival in this strange, enchanting, yet ultimately disappointing country the previous summer. Was there a difference in the city now? No, but I think I had changed. Immersing yourself in Russian culture for a year can do that to you.

I'm not exactly sure *how* I had changed, but I was pretty certain I knew *why*. Part of it was because I had finally confirmed something I had always known but hadn't experienced in its rawest form: the mighty struggle between the people — disenfranchised, desperate, despairing — and their *real* enemy, those who rule over them.

I thought I'd seen "power politics" at its worst in our country. But while the theft of votes (or even land) could be pretty raw and even deadly in our country (for proof, see *A Texan Looks At Lyndon* — or any newspaper from Chicago or Newark), it was bush-league stuff compared to what my friends in Russia have seen every day of their lives.

It made me terribly sad to see the living evidence that the greatest enemy of mankind is, always and everywhere, his own government. And to realize that, in all the best colleges all over the world, students are being taught exactly the opposite. Think of the terrible irony: Young people from some of the most repressive regimes on earth come to the United States, only to be taught that "government is your friend and is the great benefactor of its citizens."

Will we ever be able to liberate our children from this seemingly endless seduction? Will they always be taught to believe in the beneficence of government and the wisdom of the majority? I see little hope that it will change in my lifetime. (But I must admit, the November '94 elections were encouraging.)

On my return to St. Petersburg in June '93, I was presented with yet another example of the perseveration of the socialist tyranny against capitalism and freedom. Russia's "democratic" government had passed new legislation that permits private foreign ventures to pay very little tax to the state. But joint ventures — that is, those in which Russian people participate — will continue to be heavily taxed.

Also, the export tax on art work has been reduced — to "only" 100 percent. Now the artists are "equal partners" with the bureaucracy. The artist does all the work, takes all the risk, and then watches helplessly as his benevolent betters grab half the pie — just like in the U.S. No wonder I get a little discouraged and depressed, as I realize how long and difficult a road it will be for these people to ever achieve anything remotely close to real freedom.

"... the more they stay the same"

Even the weather is adding to my depression. June 21 is the summer solstice, the longest day of the year. It's the time of the glorious and magical "white nights," that giant computer screen in the sky I've described before. But this year it's just another cloudy and damp St. Petersburg night. It was a short night, to be sure, but nothing like the magic I was hoping for.

Leda and I sometimes stroll the ancient byways and alleys of St. Petersburg under the glow of the Arctic sun at three in the morning. We kiss at the Kazan Cathedral and stroll along the Neva River and Nevsky Prospekt. The street bands play "Moonlight Serenade" and "April in Paris." But I have discovered that April in Paris is not as romantic as June in St. Petersburg. Here, everybody is a little snozzled, and in love with love.

You suffer through the long, dark St. Petersburg winter anticipating your reward in summer — the sun, the warmth, the silver sky at three in the morning. This year we got nothing of the sort. My beautiful St. Petersburg summer was being continually rained out. It was like going to a wedding and being told the groom and best man had been killed on the way to the church. What a downer!

But Leda brightened the night. I had a dinner party for three American pals from Florida. They were on one of those quick-look tours Americans are famous for: "Today is Tuesday, we must be in ____." Fill in the blank. I know they were impressed with Leda, because every time she would ask them a question in her sexy, wonderfully inflected and fractured English, they spilled a little more borscht on their shirt.

They will always remember St. Petersburg as I do: a city of incomparable architecture and beautiful, sensuous women. My friends were all happily married, but I noticed they swallowed a lot. We saw them off in a taxi to their ship and then strolled the St. Petersburg streets. The weather had mercifully cleared and we were granted just a little of that magical midnight glow I longed for.

In an hour, it was gone. The shroud had returned and we noticed the cold. We quickened our pace and headed north to my apartment. This time, Leda did stay. As it turned out, she wasn't tired of me and the passion of our first St. Petersburg night returned. Russian women have their own agenda, and you can take it or leave it. If you are in love with a Russian woman, you must go with the rhythm of her heart.

But there is a wall between us. She knows I must leave St. Petersburg. Will she come with me?

Her choice seems easy to me: Come to Finland with me. "Your life there will be infinitely better than in St. Petersburg," I tell her. "There's no comparison, so what's the problem?"

From Leda's point of view, there's always a problem. Can she leave Russia? She's just learning what it means to be free.

Finland could be too much, too soon. That's probably psychological piffle, but some people think that way.

Will the Russian bureaucrats grant her a visa? It isn't certain, by any means. Socialism lives in Russia; the nomenklatur still pull the strings. If they don't want Leda to go, she can't go; it's that simple. She once worked in a top-secret manufacturing plant. Most workers in these facilities are banned from foreign travel FOR LIFE.

Later on, I spoiled the mood of magic by pleading with Leda, please come with me to Finland. She wouldn't give me reasons; just looked at her hands and said, softly, sadly, "No, Beel, it's not possible."

It *is* possible. I know it is. But I can't get her to believe it — or even to discuss it.

"Are you angry with me, Beel?"

I shook my head. We didn't talk, and soon I dozed off. When I awoke, the silver glow was gone and so was Leda. She'd left without leaving a note. My anger and frustration had wounded her, which depressed me even more.

Chapter Twenty-Nine

It's Time to Say Goodbye

I've been one year in St. Petersburg. I've watched the long winter nights loosen their grip on the city. In early March, I enjoyed awakening to sparkling snow and the return of the rooks and sparrows to their summer homes in the Peter and Paul Fortress, just a cannon shot from my apartment. The birds have the best view in the city.

Then comes April. The days are no longer dark and cold — they are BRIGHT and cold, and now comes the early-spring depression: the brightness promises spring but it isn't delivered. The birds seem optimistic — which seems something of a mockery to those of us who don't, like those birds, have the privilege of wintering in warmer climes.

A year ago, when I was still young and naive, I said that the judgment of some of my friends was too harsh in saying that what Russia really needs is to be conquered by a smarter, tougher, more civilized country. A year later, I've come to agree with them.

Despite everything I've said about "the Russian soul" and the adaptability of these people to incredible hardship, the cruel fact is that they no longer have the makings of a great civilization. The communists may have lost power (I'm still not completely convinced of that), but they won the war; that is, they succeeded in turning 300 million people into servile, dependent wards of the state. Oh, there are a few people left who don't fit the mold;

there are even some who will try to break it. But there are not enough to make a revolution; there are not enough to remake a country.

Of course, it's dangerous to generalize about a land with 120 different ethnic groups and hundreds of different languages. Forty percent of Western Russia's people aren't even Russian, but Ukrainian. In the whole country, which is four times larger than mainland U.S., there are Uzbeks, Azzeris, Kazaks, Chinese, Byelorussians, Tajiks, Georgians, Tartars, Bashkirs, Armenians, Gypsies, Koreans, Mongolians, Azerbajanies, and many little want-to-be nation-states you have never heard of, such as Bashkirskaya.

The tsars and Bolsheviks were right — there really is no way to hold this polyglot of a nation together but through ruthless dictatorship. It's the only thing that worked in the past and it is the only thing that will work in the future. Democracy is an absurdity and self-defeating under the best of circumstances. In the context of this huge collection of peoples who can't even communicate with a common language, it is a complete delusion.

It's a waste of resources, energy, and human lives to force these diverse peoples together into a common government. The dissolution process that started with the breakup of the Soviet Union must continue. Why should people in the west of Russia, led by lying politicians who promised the voters anything and everything — just like in the United States — run the affairs, about which they know nothing, of people on the Chukotski Peninsula, which is almost half a world away to the east?

It will be impossible for the drunken, half-starved Russian military to contain 120 different peoples. Only the importation of tens of thousands of UN mercenaries, at a cost of untold billions of dollars, can hold this monstrosity called Russia together. As our President has apparently developed a taste for blood (ref. Haiti, Somalia, Bosnia, Syria, et al) and no longer believes the "peace" agenda of his youth, it is not too far-fetched to think that many of the troops wearing those baby-blue UN helmets will come from our shores.

Some observers with a reflexive hatred of the United States see the present situation as a conspiracy by the U.S. to take over the world with its military, using the UN as a protective screen. In fact the opposite is true. America, along with other Western powers, is being used by the New World Order crowd to build an international military force which could someday turn on the United States — probably under the pretext of riot control, the "war on drugs," or protecting civil rights.

Who could become the first Joseph Stalin of the New World Order? Bill Clinton? Henry Kissinger? Mikhail Gorbachev? Boris Yeltsin? Some brilliant and ruthless servant of his Insider masters we don't know about today? Does it really matter?

"Until we meet again...."

I am making preparations to leave St. Petersburg. I've given away most of the odds and ends I've accumulated during my stay here. There is one wonderful table I gave to Nikolai and Galia. The top is a chess board made by two kinds of inlaid wood. It probably took some poor artisan *months* to make; I paid a hundred bucks for it. Nikolai says he will hold it for me.

I'll take my beloved Errol Garner CDs with me, of course; but many of the books I've acquired will stay behind — gifts to some wonderful Russian friends.

It now appears certain that Leda won't accompany me to Finland. I am devastated, but I cannot stay here any longer, even for her. My photobiological research is virtually done. I can leave the continuing details in the capable hands of Dr. Nikolai Chaika. I will remain close by in Finland for several months, since there will be important meetings and negotiations as we try to import their knowledge, and even some of their publications and instruments, into the United States.

And there's another reason for staying nearby — the lady with the alabaster skin and golden-chestnut hair, Leda, my lubemaya.

But I know the pitfalls of doing business, any kind of business, in Russia. There's too much history to escape here.

Westerners think capitalism can spring up whole cloth in Russia, forgetting what 70 years of communism can do to the heart and soul of a people. We expect the communist party, with its butchers and mindless bureaucrats, to simply disappear. Or that the mass murderers and mindless fools who composed its ranks will somehow suddenly see the light. I hope by now you realize these expectations are hopelessly foolish and naive.

With Leda it's the same thing. Perhaps there are too many years between us. More likely, there is just too much *life* between us. Too many experiences that were dissimilar; too many hopes and expectations we *didn't* share.

And even if we could overcome the differences between us, she is still Russian — for whatever that means, good and bad. If I'm taking anything with me from this city and this society, it's the feeling that somewhere in Russia, the other boot is always waiting to drop.

With or without Leda I must leave. Before my year in Russia, I probably would have told you that I would do whatever it takes to have Leda with me — if I were ever lucky enough to find a Leda.

Now I see that "whatever it takes" sometimes isn't enough. Too many times I've watched the Russian people give all they have and get nothing back but a boot in the face.

I'll be waiting, hoping, and praying for Leda and for this great country. But I will wait and watch from a distance.

I have no idea what the future holds. I'm optimistic, but realistic enough to know that anything can happen. Unfortunately, when it comes to Russia and her people, I've learned to hope for the best but to expect the worst.

On the other hand, maybe there will be a chance for me to return, to enjoy the rest of my "thousand and one" St. Petersburg nights. Looking back, I'm grateful for every single one I had. I wouldn't have traded this year for anything. But it's time to move on.

Postscript

Reflections on My
Strange, Enchanting Year

In December 1993, the Russians had their first "free" elections in nearly a century. To the amazement and concern of many observers, a fascist madman named Vladimir Zhirinovsky came skyrocketing onto the political scene — rattling rockets, spewing virulent anti-semitism, and promising to conquer the world.

I wasn't surprised. As this book has repeatedly emphasized, the Nazi spirit has been present in Russia ever since the October communist revolution of 1917. The KGB, as we also emphasized, has remained very much alive since "the fall of communism."

Even more alarming, the elite sabotage and assassination wing of the KGB, the GRU Special Forces known as *Spetsnats*, lies in readiness. And thanks to the Russian mafia, these deadly soldiers of darkness are in position to spread terror and sabotage across Russia and into Europe and the United States. They only await the command.

This may sound alarmist and melodramatic, but it is not. The Russian mafia, with its KGB/GRU connections, has become a serious threat to the free world. No one wants to talk about it because, at the leadership level, no one has a solution for it.

There was a funeral in Russia last year for a writer named Dima. He was trained as a reporter by his editor and mentor,

Vadim Peogli, and became the most popular reportorial freedom-fighter in Moscow.

The KGB and GRU allowed Dima wide latitude in his articles and stories, because they weren't worried about what the Russian people read. They knew the people were powerless.

But when Dima started writing about the Spetsnats forces, that was something else again. He was treading on forbidden ground. And when he wrote about the Spetsnats/mafia linkage (including evidence that Spetsnats were training mafia hit men to carry out assaults in the West), he had gone too far.

He was killed when a bomb exploded in his office. All the democratic forces in Moscow attended his funeral, with the notable exception of Boris Yeltsin. Chess grand master Gary Kasparov flew from America for the service, where he said: "This is the funeral of ... Yeltsin's union with the people.... To my mind, the unity that brought Yeltsin to power has now ceased to exist."

I'm afraid the funeral of Dima was also the funeral of hope for Russia.

Another clear sign that Russia is slipping back down the hill to socialism occurred just as this book was going to press. It seems that Vladimir Polevanov, the gentleman in charge of privatizing Russia's industries, has not only stopped any further privatization; he's gone further and called for *renationalizing* businesses that were already sold. And to make certain there was no mistaking his intent, he issued an indictment forbidding Western businessmen to set foot in any of the buildings run by the State Property Committee, which he heads.

One other point you should know: Polevanov was appointed to his post by that great democrat and born-again capitalist, Boris Yeltsin.

Liberals and other self-deluded people will be shocked to see fascism rising like a monster gorilla in Russia, blocking out the sunshine of liberty. The dreamers, the politicians, and the foolishly naive may finally see Russia as it has truly been for the past 75 years — a Nazi/fascist state that used communism as a convenient cover.

Russian fascists have been calling for "the final solution" for many years. Many Russian Jews now realize they really mean it and have decided it's time to take any vehicle moving out of the county.

Until the elections a year ago, Zhirinovsky was unknown outside Russia. But he was far from an obscure figure within his own country and, in fact, had come in third behind Yeltsin in the election that brought Yeltsin to power.

Although I have always been pessimistic about the future of Russia, I had hoped that a miracle would occur, in the form of a Pinochet or Salazar who would lead them out of their socialist-fascist straightjacket. The strong showing of Zhirinovsky indicates they are more likely to get a Mussolini than a Pinochet.

My year of good and bad

My publisher asked me what was my greatest disappointment during my sojourn in Russia. There were two: First was the discovery that my old attitudes and impressions about this pathetic place, based on 30 years of study about communism and the USSR, were absolutely correct. I can see why Boris Pasternak's great novel, *Dr. Zhivago*, was banned in Russia for so long. It was too terribly true.

And it is not much different for the Dr. Zhivagos of today. There are a lot of broken-down cars on the streets, instead of horses, but otherwise it's the same.

And second, I love the Russian people, but I am afraid there is no hope for them. The smart ones, especially the Jews who make up a high percentage of the remaining brains in the country, are getting out as fast as they can. This will cause a cultural and scientific implosion that will condemn Russia to 500 years of mediocrity. Russia's only hope is to be recolonized by Europeans (I recommend the Scots) or orientals. I'm afraid their gene pool is hopelessly depleted. It's going to take a lot of romance between Russians and capitalist foreigners to improve the race.

On the positive side, one of the most gratifying things to me personally was how protective the average Russian was toward me. The neighbors never pried, but they were quick to act if I was doing something they thought endangered my safety. One dark winter evening, I was going out to dinner at the Teblesi. I had opened the door to the unlit hall, then realized I had forgotten my wallet. I turned back to get it, leaving the door ajar. An elderly woman appeared out of the darkness and said (I caught enough words to get the meaning): "Please don't leave your door open, even for a minute. Everybody knows you are a Westerner and you could be robbed and injured."

There were many variations to that scenario, a real concern for my safety, that will cause me to feel a genuine affection for these sad people for the rest of my life.

Nikolai will soldier on, hating his country's phychotic and stupid "leaders." I've urged him and Galia to emigrate while they possibly can, before the gate closes again. They won't leave their children, although I don't think the children, grown and immersed in their own lives, really care. Nikolai is fully aware that when he is old and crippled, sick and near death, he will be forgotten and half-starved. Social Security in the U.S. may be a fraud, but it is a cornucopia compared to the way the elderly suffers in the worker's paradise. All he has to do is look out his office window at the widows of deceased military heros, even the wives of admirals and generals, lined up at the post office once a month, standing in sub-zero weather to receive a fistful of almost valueless coins or dirty paper rubles.

There is no retirement in Russia, only poverty, penury, and suffering. The only difference from your "productive" years is that you don't go to a useless job anymore and you are sick, but without any semblance of decent medical care or even relief from your pain.

And, by the way, there was a third disappointment. It was learning that the poets were wrong. Love does not always find a way.

Get a *Second Opinion* every month with Dr. Douglass' medical newsletter

Here's a shocker for you: Did you know that cancer, heart disease, the common cold, and a host of other "incurable" or "chronic" illnesses, are in many cases now completely reversible?

Did you know that garlic can help with certain forms of depression? That cabbage juice can cure the most stubborn, painful ulcer — almost immediately? That extra magnesium in your diet can reduce tendencies toward anxiety, obesity, and even heart palpitations?

It's true. And it's exactly the kind of helpful medicine that can help keep you out of your doctor's office. It'll help you live longer, feel better, even look younger. You can only find such invaluable advice in *Second Opinion*.

With *Second Opinion*, you'll see your doctor less ... spend a lot less money ... and be much happier and healthier while you're at it. Go ahead and subscribe today! When you do, we'll give you one of the reports or books described in the next two pages absolutely free ... you choose the one you want!

Choose your free book/report on the next three pages!

Don't drink your milk!

If you knew what we know about milk ... BLEEECHT! All that pasteurization, homogenization and processing is not only cooking all the nutrients right out of your favorite drink. It's also adding toxic levels of vitamin D.

This fascinating book tells the whole story about milk. How it once was nature's nearly perfect food ... how "raw," unprocessed milk can heal and boost your immune system ... why you can't buy it legally in this country anymore, and what we could do to change that.

Dr. Douglass travelled all over the world, tasting all kinds of milk from all kinds of cows, poring over dusty research books in ancient libraries far from home, to write this light-hearted but scientifically sound book. And if you like, it's yours free when you subscribe to *Second Opinion!*

The
Milk Book
How Science is Destroying
Nature's Nearly Perfect Food

You've got more to choose from! See the next two pages.

Is it possible this generations-old treatment could actually
STOP AIDS, CANCER, TUBERCULOSIS
and other killer diseases of our time?

We've seen this procedure save lives every place it has been used, from Russia to Central Africa to the practices of a handful of physicians in this country farsighted enough to use it.

What is it? It's called "photo-luminescence." It's a thoroughly tested, proven therapy that's been miraculously successful, with absolutely no dangerous side effects.

This remarkable treatment works its incredible cures by stimulating the body's own immune responses. That's why it cures so many ailments — and why it's been especially effective against AIDS!

Yet, 50 years ago, it virtually disappeared from the halls of medicine. Why has this incredible cure — proven effective against many ailments, from AIDS to cancer, influenza to allergies, and so much more — been ignored by the medical authorities of this country?

That's why Dr. Douglass wrote **Into the Light**. This hard-hitting, fully documented book tells the success story of photo-luminescence — what it can heal, who it's helped, who covered it up and why.

Get **Into the Light** now and discover the whole story for yourself.

Into the Light

You've got more to choose from!
See the next page.

Choose one of our special reports as your free gift!

AIDS: Why It's Much Worse Than They're Telling Us, And How To Protect Yourself And Your Loved Ones

Yes, AIDS is easy to catch. No, it isn't limited to just a few groups of society. People who've never engaged in questionable behavior or come within miles of an infected needle are contracting this deadly scourge. To protect yourself, you must know the truth.

Dangerous (Legal) Drugs

If you knew what we know about the most popular prescription and over-the-counter drugs, you'd be sick. That's why Dr. Douglass wrote **Dangerous (Legal) Drugs**. He gives you the low-down on 15 different categories of drugs: everything from painkillers and cold remedies to tranquilizers and powerful cancer drugs.

Prostate Problems: Safe, Simple, Effective Relief

Don't be frightened into surgery or drugs you may not need. First, get the facts about prostate problems ... know all your options, so you can make the best decisions. This fully documented report explains the dangers of conventional treatments, and gives you alternatives that could save you more than just money!

Eat Your Cholesterol

Never feel guilty about what you eat again! Dr. Douglass shows you why red meat, eggs, and dairy products aren't the dietary demons we're told they are. But beware: This scientifically sound report goes against all the "common wisdom" about the foods you should eat. Read with an open mind!

To subscribe and choose your free gift, please use the order form on the next page.